THOMA  R

REDEFINING THE
AMERICAN
DREAM

HOW TO THINK **BIG** AND GROW **RICH**

SPIRIT REIGN
PUBLISHING
A Division of Spirit Reign Communications

Author: Thomas Felder
Cover design: David Anderson
Page design & layout: Ornan Anthony of OA.Blueprints, LLC

Printed in the United States of America.

ISBN Softback: 978-1-940002-41-5
ISBN ePDF: 978-1-940002-43-9
ISBN ePUB: 978-1-940002-42-2

SPIRIT REIGN
PUBLISHING
A Division of Spirit Reign Communications

TABLE OF CONTENTS

DEDICATION

This book is dedicated to all the people who are committed to getting out of the box and living the American Dream.

ACKNOWLEDGEMENTS

Thank you TEAM TNT for always giving 1000 percent; we are just getting started.

Thank you Kamilla, Ronda, Vince, Beverly, Owen, Juan, Deon, and Darren, Tupac, Uncle Les, Stan, Steve, Damon, Swann Twins, Barry J., Ian, Chad, and Barry D. for being friends and mentors to me.

Thank you to my friend, Jay, who introduced me to network marketing and to Marty and Isra who spent countless hours educating me about residual income.

Craig, Jeb, Jason and William, thank you for your vision. Jamie and Tina, you guys are awesome.

Sis. Kathleen, Kathy, Franz, Bro. Paul Cameron, and Pastor Daryl, the prayer warriors—thank you, prayer works.

Thanks to TEAM Power & TEAM SVP Express for always pushing me to be better and do more. Thank you, Darryl, Lisa & Tillman, and Chris for your support and technical expertise.

To those on the front lines, Raynale, Cynthia, Colin and Debra, Abdirisak , Mohmed , Skip, Cedric, John & Helen, Jeff, Keith, Sokoni, Demetrius, Tracey, Phillip, Tabitha, Eric, Dr. Shay, Dr. Callwood, and Ray, and so many others who contributed to the success of the team.

Thanks to my sisters, Lynnette and Evelyn. Special thanks to my sister Denair, and nephew Shon for their incredible leadership. Thank you, Ed for inspiring and helping me write this book.

To my Amazing Mother Mary, thank you for always encouraging me to be my very best.

I want to thank my beautiful wife, Melodie, for always inspiring and supporting me. Thanks for being my best friend.

To my children, Carrington, Alexandra and Adrianna you were born to soar. Never settle for anything less than greatness. Don't stop believing.

Special thanks to my publisher, Spirit Reign Publishing and my editor, Ruthie.

Finally, I give thanks and honor to God most of all. He has proven time and time again that he will open up the windows of Heaven and pour out a blessing that there shall not be room enough to receive it.

FOREWORD

Your life does not get better by chance,
it gets better by change.
~ Jim Rohn

The entire family was thrilled to be together. It was my birthday, it was Thanksgiving, Why not kick start the best Soul Train Line ever? The only one missing was Thomas aka Tommy as the family affectionately calls him. Tommy was always arriving late to Atlanta for the family's annual Thanksgiving bash at Lynnette's house. Evelyn and Denair, my younger sisters, were bumping hips as they glided down the line. There was a faint knock on the door; no one glanced or made the slightest move toward it for fear of losing their place in the fast moving action packed soul train line....

Out of the corner of my eye I see Tommy sprinting down the hall, I watched him leap into the air like Leroy from the 1980's hit TV show *Fame*, and in one full scoop he did a spilt, bounced up and began break dancing. His timing was impeccable! His dance moves were priceless. The room exploded with cheers and laughter.

Amidst the hugs, kisses and high fives, Tommy announced to the entire family, he had shut down his law practice and that we would all be rich. He was literally bouncing off the walls. Shaking my head, I thought my brother had finally lost it!

An exuberant Tommy explained that he had come across an opportunity that would make the gold rush look like chump change. I thought Tommy was certainly Thinking Big! He was introduced to network marketing and was very excited about the possibilities it offered.

His strategy was a simple one; introduce thousands of wage earners to residual income. His last point floored me; he would do all of this from the comfort of his living room. He stated that he would lead a team of millions with a laptop and cell phone while in his bathrobe and house slippers. Would my brilliant brother who had dined with Oprah, Presidential Candidate Senator Obama, and Stevie Wonder really ruin his dream career for some two-bit opportunity?

As a former banking executive, who operated one of the top small business lending firms in the South, I was all for the little guy. Over the years, I packaged and funded deals for hundreds of ordinary Americans looking to purchase hotels, gas stations, restaurants, software firms and apartment complexes. In my opinion these were the folk living the American Dream.

As I watched my brother crisscross the country, sharing his enthusiasm and amazing opportunity, with hundreds of people in churches, school auditoriums and country clubs I began to realize … there was a shift going on in America. His once small team was now comprised of thousands of professionals—white collar and blue-collar. Like any great leader, Tommy recruited the best and the brightest to join his fledging organization. True to his word, Tommy was in the process of building a team of millions who worked 2 to 3 hours a day from the comfort of their homes. 20-year nurses and software engineers were leaving their full time jobs and earning 5-figures a month after being on Thomas's team for less than a year. People who were driving minivans and 10-year-old cars were now driving brand new silver BMWs.

He taught his team members how to Think Big, Eliminate Excuses, and Move with a Sense of Urgency; those who did so were rewarded handsomely. One guy who took the bull by the horn was a 20-year corporate executive who I'll call Joe. Joe was earning in excess of $200,000 a year on his day job. Just three weeks after joining the business Joe was called into his manager's corner office and given his pink slip. Two days after receiving his pink slip, Joe received his first network marketing check, which matched his regular salary for the same time period. Joe was on pace to be financially free in less than 2 years.

My ambitious younger brother was on to something and it was big. As he traveled the country, many people were excited about the prospect of building a residual income. The paradigm shift had been made. Ordinary Americans seeking to build wealth, those seeking to live the New American Dream could do so from the comfort of their homes, working minimum hours and earning maximum wages.

Many of my former banking clients would be closer to retirement and happier if they didn't have to work 12 to 14-hour days; if they weren't paying $5,000 to $10,000 a month in business loan payments or forced to drain their home equity to begin their entrepreneurial endeavors due to high overhead and start up costs.

As you read the pages of "Redefining The American Dream, How To Think Big and Grow Rich," I invite you to embrace the success strategies spelled out in the book. Imagine Thomas's success as your success. I challenge you to Think Big and take massive action. Greatness is in you and you deserve to win. Plant your flag and take this opportunity to Redefine Your Dreams.

"Build castles, don't dig graves."
~ David J. Schwartz, *The Magic Of Thinking Big*

Edward E. Felder, Jr. MBA

Author *"It's Money In The Bank: 7 Insider Tips To Financing Any Small Biz!"*

INTRODUCTION

What is the American Dream?

The American Dream is the traditional social principles and ideals upon which rests the foundational building blocks of the United States. Equality, democracy and material prosperity are a few of the core components of the American Dream.

However, the American Dream was not within reach in my community; it wasn't visible in my neighborhood, nor was it visible in my own home. There were times it seemed as though we were living the American nightmare. No matter how hard I tried, I could never figure out how to get a grasp on the "Dream" and claim my slice of the American Pie. I longed to taste, see and smell it. I searched high and low, near and far my entire life but it always escaped me.

My desire to live the American Dream began when I was a young boy. My life was not the picture perfect *Leave it to Beaver* type lifestyle; it was the exact opposite. I was born and raised in the South Bronx but, even so, I felt destined to not only claim the American Dream but also redefine it.

One of my favorite shows as a child was *The Adventures of Jonny Quest*. For those who may not be familiar with the TV series, it's an animated science fiction adventure about an eleven-year-old boy who accompanies his scientist father on extraordinary adventures. This show truly epitomized the essence of my cranial voyages.

The creators of the show gave *Jonny Quest* a very distinctive look, and packed the show with action and adventure unlike any other animated series on TV during the 1980s. Although *Jonny's* character was only eleven years old, he seemed to have a yearning for bigger and better things. I easily identified with *Jonny's* quest for greater things. So, at the tender age of seven, in the Bronx, N.Y., I began my own quest.

My voyage has taken me many places; from rubbing elbows with Oprah Winfrey and Bob Johnson, to General Counsel for the fourth richest county in the nation, and running my own successful law practice. I mistakenly believed I was living the American Dream but I was in for a rude awakening.

As a corporate attorney, I worked fifteen hours a day barely spending time with my family. It was dark when my workday began and it was dark when it ended. Every second was precious, I never wasted any time. It was often well after 7 p.m. when I'd get home; tired, hungry and sometimes moody. I'm generally not a moody person, but as a trial lawyer I'd have many long days in court, after which all I wanted to do was get home and settle into my nightly routine. My normal evening routine consisted of helping my kids with their homework, making dinner, checking items on my honey-do list (if you don't know what that is ask a married person), taking a quick nap and then finishing my fifteen-hour workday. When I was in my twenties this grueling routine was a breeze, but when I reached my forties this arduous schedule was merciless and exhausting. I was desperately looking to rewrite this chapter of my life.

Although I had the white picket fence and luxury cars, I was working myself into divorce and/or an early grave. I feared that working at such a hectic pace would alienate my children. I didn't want to become a stranger to them. I kept telling myself there has to be a better way not only for me but the millions of hardworking Americans struggling to live the "American Dream". Then one day, like a flash of lightning, it was clear that if I wanted a different result, I needed to embark on a new and exciting path.

I never imagined being able to retire 30 years earlier than I originally thought possible. The real prize was not only retiring myself but my wife, my mother, and five generations yet unborn. That, my friend, is what Redefining the American Dream is all about!

REDEFINING THE AMERICAN DREAM

Think big, talk little, love much.
Laugh easily, work hard, give freely, pay cash, and be kind.
It's enough...
To laugh often and much;
To win the respect of intelligent people and the affection of children;
To earn the appreciation of honest critics and to endure the betrayal of false friends;
To appreciate beauty;
To find the best in others;
To leave the world a bit better whether by a healthy child, a garden patch or a redeemed social condition;
To know even one life has breathed easier because you have lived...
This is to have succeeded.
Ralph Waldo Emerson 1803-1882

The American Dream may represent different things for different people. However, on a fundamental level, the above quotes by **Ralph Waldo Emerson** seem to capture the very essence of what each of us should aspire to achieve.

CHAPTER 1

"THE GREAT ESCAPE"

I was born poor that was not my fault,
if I die poor then that's my fault.
~ Bill Gates

It was a hot July night in 1977, I was seven years old and battling a severe bout of asthma. I clutched my chest shouting—Mommy, Mommy, Mommy ... I can't breathe! I can't breathe! I knew help was on the way because I could hear what sounded like hundreds of sirens circling the neighborhood. I was thinking they must have sent the entire New York City Fire department to come rescue me. After Dr. Mommy gave me a few blasts from my inhaler, I defied her orders and bolted to the window to see what all the commotion was about. As smoke filled the neighborhood and fire trucks raced up and down the block, I quickly realized I wasn't the emergency that brought about all the chaos and had the entire block in turmoil.

It was absolute pandemonium. I couldn't believe what I was seeing. I thought my eyes were playing tricks on me. There were hundreds of people, young and old going wild in the streets. My neighborhood was in the midst of a full-blown riot and there was nothing I could do about it.

I leaned out the window and yelled to my brother, 'I

*can't believe those bad guys and grandmas are break-
ing into the stores and walking away with refrigerators,
televisions, and toys! Oh snap, is that Mrs. Parker walking
down the street pushing a shopping cart of food?'*

I knew she couldn't afford to pay for that much food on
one welfare check. Johnny, who lived across the street,
was racing up the block with a shiny red huffy bike with
the tags still on it; while Raymond from around the corner
was sporting a really sweet yellow and blue big wheel.
It was beginning to look a lot like Christmas all over the
neighborhood, except for my front porch. Everyone was
celebrating and having a grand old party, except for
my happy-go-lucky Christian family. Thanks Mom!

Although I knew the wages of sin was death, would I really go to hell for taking a G. I. Joe action figure or a brand
new pair of tennis shoes that I desperately needed? If it
was so wrong, why were the police officers standing idly
by watching all the looting without lifting a finger to stop
it?

While the atmosphere was festive during the day, all hell
broke loose when the sun went down. The 1977 New York
City "Black Out", as it was later coined, turned my once
quiet South Bronx neighborhood into a nighttime war
zone.

Common sense was thrown out the window along with
the baby and the bath water. The South Bronx and the
entire city of New York were plunged into darkness.
Mayhem and madness quickly followed as the night was
filled with sounds of shotgun blasts, ricocheting bullets
and folks' doors getting kicked in. What I initially considered a day of amusement quickly turned into a harrow-
ing event for millions of law abiding citizens.

Can you imagine not having any water, air condition-ing, TV, or electricity for twenty-four hours? Hundreds of thousands were stuck in the rat-infested subways. The Big Apple; The City that never slept; The City that everyone wanted to wake up and find themselves king of, was days away from bankruptcy. Was this citywide power outage some kind of ploy by our local politicians? To add insult to injury, this was also during the time the city was being terrorized by the notorious Son of Sam killer. New Yorkers were pissed off and rightfully so!

With sirens blaring and the neighborhood going up in flames, I so appreciated my mother's courage under fire. To uplift our spirits and give my siblings and me a sense of calm, mom quoted Bible verses, allowed us to play footsy and invited my four older siblings and me to pile into her comfy bed to enjoy a good night's rest.

When the looting stopped and the smoke cleared, my neighborhood was all but unrecognizable! Apartment buildings that once housed hundreds became unin-habitable. Cars were flipped upside down and broken glass was everywhere. The Bronx was on fire and no one seemed to care. Where was the sense of pride? Where were the heroes when we needed them most? Gone were the white picket fences and family atmosphere. For many, the American Dream went up in flames the night the power went out.

All that was left was decay and a sense of sadness. The City reported that 550 police officers were injured, 4,500 looters were arrested and there were nearly 1,500 cases of arson. The damage done to my once proud neigh-borhood was far greater than the $430 million price tag plastered across the cover of the New York Daily News.

Within weeks of the fire, long time neighbors that I came

to know and love began a great exodus to parts unknown. Overnight it was reminiscent of a deserted ghost town you'd see on television. To my dismay, my classmates, stick ball buddies and junior detectives who I'd patrol the streets with were replaced by strangers who didn't care about my wellbeing, my family, or my neighborhood. To me the damage was incalculable. This was the day The Bronx lost its innocence.

Not long after the fires, a little-known rap crew, Grand Master Flash & The Furious Five, debuted their hit record: The Message. Lyrics such as, ***"it's like a jungle sometimes it makes me wonder how I keep from going under"***, captured the sentiment of not only my block but the entire city, and turned this dynamic song into a hood anthem. I lived in the Bronx most of my childhood; I was born there and thought I'd be there until I died. It's where my heart was and I took great pride in my birthplace. I'd walk to Yankee Stadium to see games and pay $1.50 to sit in the cheap seats better known as the bleachers. I loved the Bronx, but after that horrific day, I slowly began to renounce my devotion to the city and gradually began to lose the passion for my hood.

While our mother did her best to help Lynnette, Eddie, Evelyn, Denair and me retain our sense of dignity and pride while living in what was now considered a slum, our daddy was a non-factor. Remarkably, while my siblings and I were lauded throughout the school district for our academic excellence; routinely winning Valedictorian, Dean's List and Student of the Year honors, daddy never appeared to be in attendance or a central figure in our lives. I heard daddy was a highly decorated New York City police officer who graduated the police academy as the *Number #1* ranked recruit. Money or, should I say, the lack thereof was ripping our family apart at the seams.

My life was greatly impacted by my father; his being present and absent at the same time for most of my childhood. I'm not sure what my dad was like before I was born, but he apparently began to battle demons after my arrival on the scene.

It was disheartening to discover daddy was a rolling stone, wherever he laid his hat was his home. After dropping mom and me home from the hospital, he immediately took off for the next few weeks without so much as a hint as to when he would return. My mother was a devout woman of God, who faithfully attended church three days a week. Mom seriously considered aborting me due to her strained relationship with my father. She wanted to abort me after she discovered she had contracted another sexually transmitted disease from dear old dad. Only this time, the STD was considered life threatening for both mom and me. To mom it seemed that the devil was throwing everything imaginable to break her will and destroy her faith. Imagine being a 25-year-old wife and mother who was singlehandedly raising a 5-year-old daughter, a set of 4-year-old twins, and a toddler just a year and a half old. Then to be saddled with another bundle of "not so much joy" sent mom into a state of total despair. I'm told she cried every day of her pregnancy with me. Prior to my birth she had a special anointing service over me. She asked the Lord to shine His light on me. She asked that I be a blessing to not only her, but to the entire world. She asked that my birth restore, replenish and renew her spirit.

As usual dad didn't make the blessing ceremony. From what I understand he was battling a host of demons that plunged his life into a downward spiral. If we were going to survive what I now considered a God-forsaken neighborhood, I'd have to exceed and excel on my own.

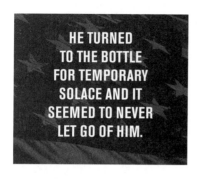

HE TURNED TO THE BOTTLE FOR TEMPORARY SOLACE AND IT SEEMED TO NEVER LET GO OF HIM.

Just months before I was born, my father's only brother, 23-year-old Thomas Wesley Felder, who I'm named after, died from an asthma attack. Around the same time of my uncle's death, my father was experiencing great turmoil on his job as a New York City police officer. After years of digging, I finally learned my dad was in the right place at the wrong time and caught a few of his superiors engaged in some "questionable activities". To quiet him and keep him in his place he was ordered to patrol the worst housing projects in New York City without any partners or back up.

Imagine chasing a suspect up twenty flights of stairs at three o'clock in the morning in areas of Harlem you'd never patrolled before, then the next day being ordered to patrol a more deadly gang-infested housing project in the Bronx. You see, it's one thing to patrol foreign terrain in a squad car sitting beside a partner, but it's a completely different story strolling some of the world's most notorious housing projects on foot with a Billy-club and flashlight as your partner. To add insult to injury, his assignments were changed at a moment's notice to keep him off-guard and guessing. When he didn't meet with an "untimely demise" the stakes were raised as he was forced out of the precinct with guns drawn. Needless to say, the former *Number #1* recruit in New York City was dishonorably discharged. I remember dad enduring an exhaustive lawsuit with the N.Y.P.D. and the City of New York. The grueling litigation, his brother's death and his lack of financial wherewithal, proved to be too much for my dad. He turned to the bottle for temporary solace and it seemed to never let go of him. Ultimately, dad's downward spiral and lack of income forced our family to remain hostages in a rapidly deteriorating hood. I could no longer call that place a neighborhood since there was nothing neighborly about it anymore.

While the more well-off families escaped Jessup Avenue for greener pastures, the F-Troop, which we affectionately called ourselves, remained swallowed up in a decaying three story brownstone like Davey Crockett at the Alamo. The property was in such dire straits and disrepair that passersby often thought the house was abandoned.

To make matters worse, once every few months, complete strangers in flat beds and pickup trucks would come peeling out from our backyard as if they were racing in the Daytona 500. Ever the adventurous one, I would rush back there to see what all the excitement was about. Without failure, I would find that the not-so-friendly neighbors were using our backyard as a dumpsite. Unwanted items such as used TV's, couches, car batteries, old stereo systems or an entire dining room set, were routinely disposed of in our backyard. There was no end to the things people tried to plunge down that ever-widening chasm in our backyard. Once someone even attempted to deposit a stolen car into the giant abyss. For all intents and purposes, my backyard had become a de facto junkyard for the neighborhood and there was nothing mom could do to stop it. What had once been an anthill suddenly became a twelve-by-three-hundred foot bottomless pit. Engineers from all over the city were baffled as to how such a ginormous hole opened up in the middle of a concrete play area in the Bronx.

The question every nosy neighbor asked was the same question that gave me great pause and caused me many sleepless nights, and the question was—*would*

the hole swallow up the house next? That possibility was particularly troubling since the bedroom I shared with my brother was at the back of the house, which was less than fifty-feet from this ever expanding sinkhole. I can't begin to tell you how difficult it was to say my prayers at night. Like most seven year olds, I would usually begin with *"Now I lay me down to sleep, I pray the Lord my soul to keep, if I should..., if I should..., if I should..."* Given my proximity to the giant crater outside my bedroom, I could never quite spit out the words *"die before I wake".* With mom looking over my shoulder, I would simply fake falling asleep or say amen before I got to that dreaded portion. I know mom left my room many a night puzzled, shaking her head thinking 'what is wrong with my boy?'

As a result of the chatter and numerous government officials sticking their noses in where they didn't belong, the City of New York condemned the yard and deemed it uninhabitable. Where would I turn now? My refuge from the plight of the neighborhood had been snatched from me. Staking my claim and planting my flag inside of the house wasn't a realistic option. While the exterior of the home looked okay the interior of my beloved home was literally falling apart brick by brick.

I'm sure you've all heard the expression—when it rains it pours, well this was literally the case in my humble abode. Whenever it rained outside, it rained inside. Imagine waking up in the middle of the night embarrassed thinking you had wet the bed, only to realize moments later that your entire bed and the bed below you was soaking wet from rain. It wasn't uncommon for my siblings and me to dodge rain drops at the kitchen table or wrap ourselves in plastic to avoid being soaked going from the dining room to the living room to watch TV.

Disappearing daddy hadn't paid the light bill, water bill, or the all-important gas bill. The furnace was in desper-

I KNEW I WAS DESTINED FOR GREATNESS BUT THIS, MY FRIEND, WASN'T IT!

ate need of repair. In an attempt to stay warm, I often went to bed fully clothed in my school uniform, mittens and coat beneath two blankets in order to battle the bone-chilling winter conditions in my bedroom. I didn't understand why I had to wear hand-me-down tennis shoes two sizes too big, and my sister Denair's tight tee shirt that exposed my bulging belly. When we were out of toilet paper, it was second nature for me to simply ball up the daily newspaper, rub it together for about forty-five seconds or until it was soft, and then wipe with it. Who lives like this? I wondered.

I was becoming increasingly fed up with racing across town battling adults with funky attitudes and funkier odors for a seat on a crowded bus that was going nowhere fast. If the bus was delayed in traffic or the boss man was in a particularly good mood and paid my father and his crew earlier than expected (roughly about 4:00 p.m.), my family and I would be up a creek without a paddle for the next seven days. You see, if daddy got his hands on that check before my brother, Eddie, and I made it to the job site, the money would be spent on booze and broads, and we wouldn't see the old man for at least another week or two. I knew I was destined for greatness but this, my friend, wasn't it!

Being an avid reader, I often found myself in the library buried in magazines and books about wealthy lawyers, bankers and stockbrokers who lived and played a stone's throw away in Manhattan's luxury condos. I was green with envy at the very thought of kids my age traveling to Walt Disney World or enjoying weekends at their country homes while I had to stash day-old bread just to insure I would be able to eat a peanut butter and jelly sandwich later on in the week.

This wasn't God's plan for me; this wasn't a part of the American Dream I'd fallen in love with from a distance. Every time I stepped foot out of the library, I'd turn to my left and see the skyscrapers of upper Manhattan. Like Robinson Crusoe, Lewis & Clark, and Marco Polo, I wanted to explore and experience a whole new world. I was done studying for exams by flashlight because we had no power due to non-payment of the bill.

Why shouldn't I enjoy the good life too? I was the top student in my third grade class. I was well-read and a great motivator. Why did I have to go to bed hungry night after night? Why wasn't there ever enough orange juice to go around? I was frustrated with being dragged to the basement and thrown in the dryer day after day. I'd twirl and tumble around for what seemed like hours. Even with the annoying reverberation of the dryer echoing in my head, I could still hear my siblings bellowing.

Then the immortal words of Popeye the Sailorman came to mind. I, too, reached a point where I shouted, *"That's all I can stands and I can't stands no more"*.

PRINCIPLE 1 - TAKE ACTION

There are 2 types of people in this world: The first type of person complains but does nothing. The second type of person takes massive action!

It was time to take action! I decided I would escape all the injustice by leaving that God-forsaken house and moving on to greener pastures where my soul would be restored and I'd finally live the American Dream. So, over the next five days I began preparing my escape. I laid it out as follows:

Sunday - Compile a to-do list.

Monday - Empty Lynnette's plastic piggy bank. She was the oldest, meanest and stingiest, and I knew she would have more than enough money for me to begin my journey.

Tuesday - Break into the twins' piggy bank. I discovered Lynnette was poorer than she let on. Note to self: Believe only half of what you hear when it comes to people bragging about their wealth.

Wednesday - Immediately after school I snuck into our spider and roach infested basement in search of old Christmas toys that might contain the double-D Duracell batteries needed for the flashlight I often used to study with. I was in and out of that dungeon in a flash without making a sound. Mission accomplished!

Thursday - Prepare and pack a meal fit for a king.

I wondered if I'd be missed by my older siblings who treated me like Joseph's brothers (in the Bible) treated

> **I WAS DETERMINED TO TAKE MATTERS INTO MY OWN HANDS AND BECOME A CLASSIC AMERICAN SUCCESS STORY.**

him. I highly doubted that. I was fortunate they hadn't already auctioned me off for thirty pieces of silver. My departure would be for the best. My only regret would be leaving the world's most awesome and incredible mom. However, with her illness that was indirectly caused by my father, I figured she would be better off without me slowing her down. I planned to return rich and famous, buy her the dream home she so rightly deserved, and treat her like the queen she was. I was determined to take matters into my own hands and become a classic American success story.

It was time for me to take action. As I slipped out of my bed fully clothed in my pursuit of happiness, a rash of old clichés flooded my little brain and gave me comfort. The first saying was: *"Ain't nothing to it but to do it."* The next was: *"There's no better time than the present."* The final one that just came from out of nowhere was: *"There's no need to fear, Underdog is here."*

As I maneuvered past my not so alert guard dog, Sport, I quietly pulled out my trusty flashlight so I could avoid stubbing my toe or tripping over any toys. I gingerly sprinted down the sixteen steps and slipped past door number two. This would be easier than taking candy from a baby. One more lousy door and five more steps and I'd be scot-free. Yes, I got out of the house undetected! I thought maybe I would go into law enforcement or become a smooth criminal. The world was my canvas, and I was going to adorn it as I saw fit.

As my bottom foot left the last step outside, I was slapped in the face with the most frigid blast of wind imaginable.

Dammit man, I scurried back up the porch to regroup. The weather outside was unreal. This temperature had to be in the single digits. Leave it to me to execute my great escape on the coldest day of the year. I manned up and told myself, I wasn't stopping now, so I leaped all five steps in a single bound. I immediately turned right and walked for what seemed like an eternity.

I had taken that path a thousand and one times, yet everything seemed so unfamiliar and strange. The abandoned apartment buildings with the broken glass panes and wide open doors seemed scarier than ever. Why hadn't I ever noticed those frightening howling sounds before? Hold up! Is that someone watching me from inside that vacant house? No... no I must've just been tripping. Every passing stray cat put me on pins and needles. Then I got the bright idea to just walk in the middle of the street so as to avoid any bad guys or rats hanging around the perimeter of the building. Yeah, that was a good plan.

After successfully making it to the highway overpass, I breathed a sigh of relief. 'Yeah boy!' I thought, 'nothing but smooth sailing from here on out.' As I was easing on down the road I began to whistle the theme song from the old Andy Griffith TV show. I was thinking, maybe this wasn't such a bad idea after all. I found myself blurting out the phrase: *"Drastic times call for drastic measures."* Yes, I should have taken these steps earlier. Then before I could spit out my next word I had come face to face with Featherbed Lane. The game plan was to make a left on Featherbed Lane and head toward the interstate that led to the George Washington Bridge that would take me to Manhattan. I had planned that route in my head for nearly a week. I planned to follow the same path George Washington and his army used to escape the British Army during the American Revolution. The Redcoats were ordered to destroy The Bronx, and

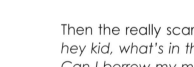

by all accounts it was a very real possibility since George Washington and his troops were outnumbered. Legend has it that local farm wives laid thousands of pounds of feathers up and down Featherbed Lane to help General Washington and his troops avoid detection by the Redcoats who were closing in on them fast. If not for the heroic efforts of the women on this street, suffice it to say, this country might not be one nation under God.

As I made a left onto Featherbed Lane, an avalanche of fear and anxiety swept over me. In stark contrast to the relative quiet and emptiness on Jessup Avenue, Featherbed Lane had as much foot traffic as Times Square during morning rush hour. I wondered what in the world all these seedy looking characters were doing on the street at three o'clock in the morning. I knew they weren't regular shoppers because 75% of the stores on that street including the corner pharmacy, the kids shoe store, and the grocery store burned down eight months earlier during the black out. Other than the ever popular liquor store, every other retail establishment on the block was chained and boarded up.

Then the really scary stuff started. I heard, *"Psst... Psst... hey kid, what's in the back pack? You're awfully cute. Can I borrow my money back? What are you doing on my street? Hey, I'm talking to you! Don't ignore me kid! I ought to!"* One really mean-looking thug shouted, *"Hey kid, isn't that my change jingling in your pocket?"* The whole scene was surreal. It was as if I was in a twilight zone movie but when I opened my eyes I realized it wasn't a dream and I wasn't in my living room watching television. I was surrounded by pimps with pistols in their waistbands and scantily clad prostitutes who offered to be my new best friend for the night. I quickly realized I was in over my head. I thought maybe if I avoided direct eye contact and kept walking briskly, I'd blend in with the crowd. All of a sudden out of nowhere, I felt some guy stick his hand in my pocket.

I bolted to a nearby phone booth and slammed the door behind me. I discovered I had dropped my flashlight so all I was armed with were three peanut butter and jelly sandwiches and fifteen dollars in coins. Scared out of my wits, I called home and pleaded with my mother to come rescue me. My mother was understandably stunned and a bit dazed at that hour of the morning. She believed I was some prankster impersonating her seven-year-old son. She was furious. She put me on hold and went to my bedroom to make sure the practical joker on the phone wasn't her son. She returned a few minutes later screaming at the top of her lungs; "Tommy, where are you?" She shouted. After she was able to regain her composure, she again asked where I was and wanted to know if I had been kidnapped. As my back was pressed against the glass phone booth, I explained to her that I ran away from home but changed my mind about the whole thing and needed her to pick me up immediately!

I was dumbfounded by what happened next. In the calmest voice my mother began asking me questions that, to me, seemed very strange considering the situation. She asked, *"Why did you leave?"* ... *"How did you get the money for this phone call?"*... *"Did you lock the door after leaving the house?"*

All the while I was thinking, *'With all due respect, lady, I'm in a life and death situation and in no mood to play twenty questions.'*

Being a Christian woman, my mother quietly prayed with me. Then she told me that since I was bold enough to run away in the middle of the night in subzero snowy weather, I was old enough to find my way home.

...*"IF AT FIRST YOU DON'T SUCCEED TRY AGAIN"!*

I was thinking, *'She's absolutely lost it and she is going to kill me if I make it home alive. Great, I'm going to die either way tonight.'* This was not how I envisioned my great escape going down. As I continued dropping coins in the pay phone to keep the operator from disconnecting this important call, my Spidey senses or future lawyer skills begin to kick in.

I was between a rock and a hard place and I knew I had to negotiate a peaceful surrender. No way was I going to face mom without a plea deal in place. I suggested that we let bygones be bygones if she agreed not to take any punitive action; by that I mean deliver the spanking of my life. Needless to say, my first stab at lawyering didn't go as planned. Every argument I presented to avoid a spanking was overruled and deemed inadmissible in my mother's court of law.

After exhausting all arguments and most of my coins, I finally decided to wave the white flag and return home if mom promised to withhold her belt and her wrath until after carefully listening to my side of the story. After laying out the reasoning behind my failed quest for liberty I was almost certain I would get away with the crime of the century. First things first, I would have to navigate the pimps, burned out buildings, and avoid the Son of Sam killer who, for all I knew, was still terrorizing the streets.

When I came back home I felt like a complete and utter failure. What I thought were reasonable requests and a sound argument fell on deaf ears. After receiving the whipping of the century I was ordered grounded until I was eighteen.

My hopes, dreams and aspirations for a new and better life had literally been crushed, compliments of a size 36-inch leather belt. My quest to be heard, to matter and to live the American Dream would not die easy though. Like Jefferson Davis, I, too, vowed to rise again. I had a date with success and I could not keep her waiting. My motto going forward would be a simple one..."If at first you don't succeed try again"!

CHAPTER 2

"BRICK BY BRICK"

OUT OF THE FRYING PAN AND INTO THE FIRE

I was still temporarily bummed out about the Great Escape fiasco, and even though I had a hearty supply of egg on my face, I quickly resolved to put it behind me; and that's exactly what I did.

When life served me lemons, I made lemonade. If someone threw a lemon at me, I would say 'thank you' and use it as motivation to move onward and upward. I didn't have the time or the inclination to wallow in self-pity and pain, or make excuses. I had bigger fish to fry right in my own house; namely, my big sis, Lynnette. I quickly surmised that if I was smarter than the smartest person I knew, and if I worked harder than the hardest worker I knew, then I would be a shoo-in to be a millionaire in no time at all. The American Dream would be mine after all.

Although I couldn't hold a note or sing a lick, I would bounce around the house singing that song from the old Annie Oakley movie:

> Anything you can do,
> I can do better.
> I can do anything
> Better than you.
> No, you can't.

Yes, I can. No, you can't.
Yes, I can. No, you can't.
Yes, I can,
Yes, I can!

Anything you can be
I can be greater.
Sooner or later
I'm greater than you.

PRINCIPLE #2 - ONWARD AND UPWARD

Regardless of what happens, keep pressing forward: The person who never stops pressing forward continues to open new doors to new opportunities.

While I was having a blast formulating my new wealth strategy, my four siblings thought I had gone mad. I'm sure they assumed I had lost a few marbles as a result of my terrible spanking. Over and over I'd sing that song. When I got tired of singing it, I'd whistle it. When I was done whistling it, I'd hum it. If looks could kill, I'd be dead. I could tell by their facial expressions what they were thinking. I knew they were wishing they could throw little Joseph [me] back in the dryer again. But nope, that wasn't happening anytime soon. I spilled the beans about them dropping me in the spin cycle and Mommy put a stop to that little game quick, fast, and in a hurry. For now, my mission impossible was to beat Lynnette in everything she did—beginning with school work. While my other siblings were academically head and shoulders above the majority of their classmates, Lynnette was my primary target since she had just been named Valedictorian at her sixth grade graduation.

After Lynnette's rousing speech in front of hundreds of parents and well-wishers, I immediately ran up to my mom before she had a chance to congratulate Lynnette and said; *"It's nice that Lynnette won valedictorian, but I'm going to win double valedictorian."* I had no idea what a valedictorian was or the requirements to become one. For all I knew it could have been a terminal disease and they were giving her flowers while she was still alive. I did, however, know Lynnette received a hundred on nearly every exam. If she had a one-hundred average then my goal was to achieve a one-hundred and one average. Nothing else mattered.   Anything short of that goal was unacceptable.

PRINCIPLE #3 - SET THE MARK

You should always have a certain marker for success and goals: Finding someone who has the success you want, and having a secret competition with them is powerful. If you never set your mark, you'll never beat your mark.

Although Lynnette was four grades higher than me, I had a distinct advantage over her in the competition because she was unaware of how fully engaged I was in the contest. In no time at all I would out-scholar the scholar. I was so excited I could barely contain myself. I felt like a kid in a candy store on Christmas Eve; everything was going my way. After a year of straight trouncing Lynnette, I spilled the beans to Mom. I told her Lynnette and I were in a competition and Lynnette wasn't as smart as she thought. Mom was furious at the thought of us wagering on academics. She wanted to know if any money was exchanged. Then she asked how long these shenanigans had been going on.   After yelling for

Lynnette to join us in the room, Mom announced there would be an immediate end to the foolishness. God wouldn't be pleased and neither was she.

Prior to Lynnette bursting into the room, I hopped on Mommy's lap and confessed that Lynnette was an innocent bystander in this game of—*anything you can do I can do better.*   Before I dug a deeper ditch for big sis, I told Mommy that Lynnette was only my measuring stick for academic excellence. I further explained that Lynnette had no idea I was competing against her and she certainly wasn't competing against me.

Whenever Lynnette received an A on a math exam, I buckled down and got an A as well. If Lynnette received an A in chemistry, I tripled the time I spent studying science and received an A as well. If Lynnette wrote a ten-page report and received an Excellent, I'd write a twenty-page paper and achieve an Excellent as well. Since Lynnette won Valedictorian, four years later I, too, won Valedictorian.

I am so grateful that my older sister was such an incredible role model for me to imitate, both in and out of the classroom. Without her constant push toward greatness I might not have become the scholar who graduated in the top one-percent of my elementary school, middle school, high school, college, and law school. What I regret most is that I wasn't able to walk across the very same stage Lynnette walked across as Valedictorian, and I never told her she was my academic hero.

One day, I stumbled upon an elderly lady who was building a concrete wall by herself. I said to myself, this might be an opportunity to earn a few extra dollars. I extended my hand and my charming 9-year-old smile and said, *'Hello, my name is Thomas Wesley Felder.'* I told her I was a future attorney who would love the opportunity to help her construct this great wall. She asked if I was a good worker, I said, *'Yes ma'am.'* Then she asked if I lived in the neighborhood. I pointed in the direction of my home. She wanted to know if I had any experience in the construction industry. I wanted to say yes, but then Grandma Felder's favorite saying rushed into my head: *"Tell the truth and shame the devil."* So, I followed grandma's advice and told the truth. I told her I was a fast learner and she wouldn't regret her decision if she chose to hire me. I suspect she already knew I didn't have any prior experience in construction but wanted to hear my response.

Congratulations, you're hired, Attorney Felder! While I was ecstatic inside, I kept it under control long enough to turn on my lawyering skills and negotiate what I considered a sweetheart deal. Five cents a brick! For five cents, I would take the brick, hammer off the old stuck-on cement, and then deliver the brick ready to be refitted for her purpose. The only thing holding me back from following in the footsteps of the Rockefellers was the lack of a car, a few thousand spare bricks and a little muscle. Hmm ... game on! I would substitute the car with a shopping cart from the grocery store; there was an unlimited supply of bricks around the neighborhood as a result of the dozens of apartment buildings that were demolished; and, my 13-year-old brother, Eddie, would be the muscle. I had everything I needed.

Within a matter of weeks, I was a full-fledged entrepreneur making money hand over finger. Before I was muscled out of my leadership role by the help aka "Eddie", I had earned somewhere in the neighborhood of $500.00. I really liked this entrepreneurial thing. My brother, Eddie, eventually out maneuvered me and became the key man on the deal. Although I lost my brick firm in his hostile takeover, I'd fallen in love with being self-employed.

Note to self: In the future, keep an eye on the muscle and negotiate a non-compete clause next time around. Money, power and financial freedom, this was without a doubt the wrong time to break huddle. Leaving my cash cow opportunity behind would be difficult. However, since we'd be moving on up to a deluxe apartment in the sky, things would pan out. At least, that's what I hoped would happen.

On D-day I was surprised we only took a few bags each. Staying in a furnished two-bedroom unit meant we would have to leave every toy, bike and meaningful piece of furniture behind. No more familiar beds, TV's, or teachers. Everything I was prepared to sweat, bleed and die for was crammed into a single plastic glad bag. To me, there was nothing glad about this situation. It was as if my whole life, up to that moment, meant nothing.

One of my last memories of 1468 Jessup Avenue was staring at the frozen fish tank in the living room and wondering how cold it must have been for the gold fish to freeze to death in the tank. If you can envision what a frozen bottle of water looks like after seven straight days in the freezer, then you'll have a pretty good idea what the ten-gallon fish tank looked like. In all honesty, the fish looked like a scientific experiment frozen in a solid block of ice. If you'd like a realistic experience of the conditions we lived in, I'd simply suggest you open your freezer, place your bare hands in there and leave them there for sixty minutes.

With the boiler down every other week and little to no money to repair it, those were the conditions we showered, ate, studied and enjoyed family time in. I can't tell you how often we ran in the house blowing our breath at each other. As kids we didn't really appreciate how grave the situation was. Children are natural survivors.

> **DURING THIS PERIOD OF UNREST, I WAS STILL SPREADING MY ACADEMIC WINGS.**

My siblings and I were definitely troopers. If we could excel living in those conditions, nothing would prohibit us from being the new standard bearers of the American Dream. NOTHING!!!

PRINCIPLE #4 - NEVER SETTLE

Successful people go into the world and change their environments. They are driven to constantly develop new ideas and not settle for the status quo.

When my sisters and Mom fell critically ill, about a year later we were whisked away to begin the next chapter in our lives. During this period of unrest, I was still spreading my academic wings. In the meantime, the housing conditions on Jessup Avenue became so unbearable that the New York City Department of Child Welfare Services approved an emergency voucher for us to leave the Bronx. The City moved us into a hotel on the Upper Westside of Manhattan. I was leaving behind the only life I'd known. The irony of the situation was that just a few years earlier I had bolted from that joint in the dead of night. However, this time as I was packing my bag, I was filled with regret and a sense of emptiness. I was the king of the hill or at least my small section of the block... really I was. I had earned a reputation as a fun kid, creative entrepreneur, and fierce competitor.

As we drove down the Westside highway and eventually past Central Park, we marveled at the green grass, families walking together and the overall wealth in the area. There were pretty little dogs running all around, a group of people tossing a football, and really nice boutiques and coffee shops. I was utterly amazed how carefree and happy everyone looked especially with it being wintertime in the Big Apple. All the buildings had doormen and awnings to protect you from the rain as you stepped outside the building. As we cruised the final few blocks, I imagined our doorman who I'd name, Alfred, calling me Master Thomas.

There was talk that we might walk down to Central Park and possibly go ice-skating during the upcoming weekend. We certainly needed and deserved a little R&R, so why not live a little.

As Granddad Rodgers rounded the corner and pulled up to what appeared to be an older warehouse, I thought he was just stopping briefly to update his directions. When he announced we'd reached our final destination and said, welcome home, my bottom lip nearly hit my knee. There must be some mistake, Pops! This couldn't be the correct location. We were the Felders and we were supposed to be parking in front of a deluxe high rise. By the look of the residents outside, the only thing high about this place were the fellas standing out front sipping on beverages from brown paper bags.

The first thing that came to my mind was, *"Out of the frying pan and into the fire"*.

What we thought was a deluxe apartment in the sky was actually a welfare hotel that housed the worst of the worst. Our New York City welfare hotel was funky, scary and dangerous. Overrun by rats, roaches, bugs, & crime. This was no place to raise a family with young kids. We eventually settled in to our fourth-floor suite, but things never really felt like home—or at least what I expected a home to look, smell and feel like. The beds reeked of urine, and there were more than enough stains on the comforters, mattresses and box springs to validate what those foreign substances were. No DNA tests needed here! Mom never allowed the sheets or blankets to touch the floor because she feared doing so would make it easier for the rats that chewed through the wall to climb up into the bed.

One way the self-employed (street entrepreneurs) who lived in the hotel earned a little extra cash was by posing as food delivery personnel. If there was a knock on your door and no one responded in a reasonable amount of time, the fake delivery person would kick your paper-thin door in and completely ransack your unit in search of valuables. Maybe it's just me, but it seemed as though it would make better financial sense to rob millionaires rather than dollar-aires ... I'm just saying!

To ensure our safety while we were in our unit, Mom constantly stacked chairs and boxes against the door. Needless to say, even with our makeshift security system in place, I still slept with one eye open. I have to believe that if the NYC Housing Authority had known about the horrific living conditions in that place, they would have shut it down and forced the slum-lord owners to reim-burse them for the outrageous fees they were charging. Even though I hoped and prayed for a speedy depar-ture from that hell hole, I was completely floored and caught off guard when I learned we were being evicted after just six months. After overhearing one of Mom's calls, I learned that this particular facility only allowed residents to stay there for six months or less. So, where would we go?

With little time and limited cash, Mom gathered Lynnette,

Eddie, Evelyn, Denair and myself around the kitchen table and prayed. She laid out a strategy that would separate our family for an undetermined amount of time. My soul cringed and my eyes watered at the thought of not being around my best friends.

Eddie would move miles away to Aunt Justine's apartment in the Soundview projects. This was particularly scary since Auntie was borderline crazy after having a bottle broken over her head by her boyfriend some thirty years earlier. During previous visits to Aunt Justine's place, I discovered she talked to herself, paced all night, and threatened to shoot any nigger that crossed her path. Whenever she left the house it was a huge sigh of relief. It gave me a chance to search for the gun she was always threatening to use on us and the neighbors.

Evelyn would stay with Grandma Felder in her one-bedroom apartment in the Castle Hill section of the Bronx. By all accounts, Evelyn made out pretty good. Grandma's house was clean, it had plenty of food, and her new high school was only a fifteen-minute bus ride away.

Lynnette, Denair, Mommy and I, started out living with Aunt Joyce in the Melrose housing projects. Melrose was one of the most vicious, crime-infested projects in all of New York City. Aunt Joyce was an absolutely gorgeous lady who closely resembled my mother. She was a kind Christian woman who opened her doors and gave what she had. While I loved spending time with my favorite cousin, Reese, I was freaked out by the multitude of roaches in the apartment.

One thing that I found really odd was the fact that my disappearing daddy began popping up everywhere I turned in those projects. I'd see him in the grocery store, walking past the basketball court, in the lobby of Aunt

Joyce's building, slipping through the side entrance of the building. Although he wasn't among our family members staying with Aunt Joyce, I was seeing him more than I had in years. After putting together a comprehensive brief, I came to the conclusion that dad had at least one other lady friend and at least one other undocumented child living in the same building as Aunt Joyce.

I wanted my family back together and yet things were unraveling very quickly. Any one of us could be displaced and forced to live with any one of my seven aunts throughout the city. I longed to be with my brother and sisters. I didn't understand. Why did we have to be separated? What was our great sin? There were no cell phones, high-speed internet, or video blogs during that time, so staying connected was particularly difficult. We often laughed about sending messages via pigeon or smoke signals. In the midst of all the confusion and relocating, there were many times I had no idea where my family was staying. Between our commuting all over the city for school and our heavy study schedules, we were growing apart. Not being able to hug or say I love you to my siblings on a nightly basis was earthshattering to me. We genuinely liked each other; no, we loved each other.

The madness we were going through was so different from our lives together on Jessup Avenue before our dispersion and displacement. Back then, Mommy would pray with us and make sure we were resting comfortably in our own individual beds. After which, we would sneak out of our rooms, hop into each other's bed, then we'd play, talk and shout all night long. Mom was often perplexed as to why we were dead tired in the morning after going to bed at 7:30 p.m. the previous evening. During that agonizing period of separation, there were many days when the only way I got to speak with Mom was via phone. She always cried when this happened and I was always hurt by her tears. Without a shadow of a doubt, Mommy's hurt from being apart from us was peeling back the fabric of all our lives.   No mas... No mas... No mas... No More. I couldn't take it anymore.

Why did God allow so many cruel things to happen to my good God-fearing family? Nevertheless, when I was at my lowest, I found comfort in the many Bible verses Mom taught us during our daily 5:00 a.m. worship service.

PRINCIPLE #5 - ACTIVATE YOUR FAITH

It's easy to have faith when things are going good, but the challenge is to activate your faith while you're in the struggle. It was in these times of my life that I had to hold on to the Word of God.

One of the scriptures I found most comforting during that trying time was Psalms 23 which reads:

The LORD is my shepherd; I shall not want.
He maketh me to lie down in green pastures,
He leadeth me beside the still waters.
He restoreth my soul,
He leadeth me in the paths of righteousness for His name's sake.
Yea, though I walk through the valley of the shadow of death,
I will fear no evil for Thou art with me;
Thy rod and Thy staff they comfort me.
Thou preparest a table before me in the presence of mine enemies
Thou anointest my head with oil; my cup runneth over.
Surely goodness and mercy shall follow me all the days of my life,
And I will dwell in the house of the LORD forever.

After being separated from my family for what seemed like an eternity, Mommy received the call we'd all been waiting for. The New York City Housing Authority had approved us for a four-bedroom, two-bath subsidized apartment in the Webster Avenue Projects. When we got the word, we jumped and shouted like rock stars. Based on our euphoric reaction, you would have sworn we'd won the lottery or a year's stay at the Ritz Carlton. I am certain that no one ever entered life in the projects with such joy and jubilation.

Ironically, this was the same New York City Housing Authority that my dad was suing. This was the same organization that was partly responsible for my family's collapse. Oddly enough, the projects, which had been our source of pain was now our saving grace.

We were literally on cloud nine for the first year we lived in the twenty-one-story tenement that housed nearly 1,200 people. It didn't matter to us that the elevators were occasionally broken and we had to climb nine flights of pissed-soaked stairs or step over the occasional drunk or dope fiends to get to our oasis in the sky. We were together, that's what mattered. The nightly shootings and weekly hallway robberies never killed our enthusiasm. Okay, maybe we were a bit rattled after Mommy and Evelyn were robbed at gun-point in the elevator. Another blow that threw us for a loop was finding a nine-millimeter bullet hole in our 9th floor living room wall. Okay, were they really that bad of a shot that their bullet made it through our wall on the 9th floor? We praised God that no one was hurt or harmed and we kept it moving.

To the right of us, as far as the eye could see, there were buildings just like ours. Our lifestyle and surroundings closely resembled that of the Evans family on the 1970's TV show, *Good Times*. When they didn't have heat or hot

WE WERE THE HAPPIEST GROUP OF POOR KIDS YOU'D EVER MEET.

water, we didn't have heat or hot water. When their toilet backed up, our toilets backed up. When they were poor, hungry and scrounging for food, we were doing the same. To be completely honest with you, we were living the life talked about in their theme song ... *keeping our head above water, making a way when we could.* Between the temporary layoffs of disappearing dad, we seemed to always be scratching and surviving.

Just fifty feet behind our apartment ran the express train from Long Island to Wall Street. We often laughed about how it had to be an express train since there was no way those privileged commuters could survive in this neighborhood. We didn't complain when the jolting of the train shook the building or the fact that the blaring noise was loud enough to wake the dead. Nope, we were the happiest group of poor kids you'd ever meet.

While others moving into the projects might have cried, *"Woe is me,"* or blame *"the Man"* and succumb to the streets, Mom wasn't having any of that. We walked, talked, dressed and acted as though we lived in Buckingham Palace. Don't get me wrong, we weren't cocky or arrogant; we just believed our greatness wasn't measured by our address. Each of us had tons of friends; we were probably one of the most popular families in the entire neighborhood.

You see, after what we'd been through on Jessup Avenue; being homeless and then terrorized in the welfare hotel, we became more grateful and more humble. We were the most closely knit family you could ever imagine.

> **AS A CHRISTIAN, I FELT OBLIGATED TO HELP THOSE NEEDY AND LESS FORTUNATE.**

On weekends our apartment was packed with dozens of kids from all over the city. Kids from church, kids from the neighborhood, and kids from school. It seemed everyone wanted to be connected and spend time with the Felders. I was tickled that our well-off friends who lived in two-parent households preferred spending nights and weekends in our ghetto apartment rather than in their Upper Westchester or Queens homes.

We'd spend hours upon hours playing Checkers, Connect Four, Scrabble, Uno, Jacks and dozens of other board games. My palace in the sky was literally a place of comfort and joy for friends who were lonely and hurting. Mom made sure everyone was well fed. She'd share a favorite scripture, and see that everyone got home safely. The power of a praying family is the mightiest source of inspiration a kid can have.

During my formative years, I learned to laugh and allow others to share in my laughter. One of the most amazing principles my mom taught me is that it's better to give than to receive. Armed with this powerful lesson, I began to work with my mother and my church in an outreach program that fed and clothed homeless men and women who slept inside Grand Central Station. Located in Midtown Manhattan, Grand Central Station is one of the busiest and most majestic train stations in the world. The station was built in 1871 by railroad magnate Cornelius Vanderbilt and is a historical landmark.

At least one million people pass by the station every day. The station is extraordinary; it has ceilings boasting beautiful artwork, marble staircases, and seventy-five feet high windows. Its architecture easily rivals the architecture of the Vatican and the Sistine Chapel.

Despite the wealth and opulent surroundings, the station involuntarily housed more than 2,000 homeless residents every night. There were literally hundreds of homeless men hiding in plain sight. As a Christian, I felt obligated to help those needy and less fortunate. Honestly, my greatest urge to help the homeless came from my shared nexus of helplessness. I was able to identify with their plight and envisioned myself being one of them. So, I extended the same kindness to them that I would want if life handed me the same cup.

Every Saturday evening my mom and I prepared food for hundreds of people using pots and pans the size of outdoor garbage cans. We would leave home around 4:00 a.m. and feed the homeless at Grand Central Station from 5:00 a.m. to 6:00 a.m. every Sunday. Upon my arrival to the station I would head deep into the tunnels to find those who were hunkered behind the train platforms, usually some 500 feet down the tracks. I wasn't afraid of the homeless; I was formerly one of them. The rats, well... that was another story.

My mother would use her last dime to buy food for the homeless. She gave new meaning to the phrase, *"give til it hurts."* Over the years, my homeless ministry began to flourish and take on a life of its own. One day, I almost went home naked. First, I took off my coat and gave it to an elderly man in distress. Then, I took the shoes off my feet and gave them to a guy wearing duct-taped cardboard Nikes. I thought I'd be in hot water with Mommy but, surprisingly, she embraced me and started to cry. She said to me, *"you do understand what it's about."* I can't say I fully understood what she meant but I was glad I didn't get in trouble with her for doing what seemed right and just made sense.

PRINCIPLE # 6
IT'S BETTER TO GIVE, THAN TO RECEIVE

This principle needs no explanation. It's actually in the Bible, found in Acts 20:35.

If more people gave, the world would be a much better place. Since I knew what it felt like to be without, I always had a giving spirit.

Before long, our homeless ministry had two sixteen-passenger vans going out every Sunday morning. One van delivered food and the other distributed shoes, coats and essentials such as, hats, gloves, scarfs and socks. Mom and I were so grateful to be serving the homeless. Then, the New York City Police started pushing us from spot to spot and finally out of the area, because so many of the underground people were congregating. There was no problem as long as they stayed out of sight deep in the tunnels. I'm hopeful that conditions have since improved for the city's homeless.

CHAPTER 3

"THE YOUNG ENTREPRENEUR"

When I think back to the time we spent in the Webster projects, I'm reminded of one of my favorite hymns, *Great is Thy faithfulness*. The chorus is most meaningful:

> *Great is Thy faithfulness, Great is Thy faithfulness*
> *Morning by morning new mercies I see,*
> *All I have needed Thy hand hath provided,*
> *Great is Thy faithfulness, Lord, unto me!*

If you don't know the entire song, I would suggest finding it on YouTube. I guarantee you'll find this classical hymn to be one of the most encouraging, inspirational and powerful songs you've ever heard.

If it wasn't for my mother's faithfulness and constant religious vigilance, I am certain my siblings and I would be street-hustlers, drug addicts, or dead by now. While I continued to excel academically, I wasn't always the goody- two-shoes Mom thought I was.

Before entering high school, I smoked some real and fake marijuana. I'm sure you know what the real stuff is, but the fake marijuana was crushed tea leaves that we rolled in pieces of brown paper shopping bags and smoked. We tore the brown bags into four-inch strips, wet the ends with a sponge and commenced smoking. I was like Sitting Bull smoking on a peace pipe.

I MADE A MENTAL NOTE TO ALWAYS IDENTIFY AMAZING LEADERS AND MIRROR THE VERY BEST IN THEM.

My run at drugs ended as fast as it began. I had asthma and the smoke was killing me. It didn't taste good either, and I burned my hands more times than I can remember. I came, I saw, I conquered. I quickly lost interest. I tasted beer, and that too was short lived. I spied out some Colt 45 beer that my dad left in the fridge. I thought the beer would taste like apple juice; it tasted like piss. After drinking the piss, I was done with all of it. Mom would never have to worry about me doing any type of drugs. I was self-regulated, no parental interference necessary. On a side note to Mom—sorry you're finding out about my indiscretions this way. Trust me, it didn't last long enough for you to even break a sweat.

Despite every obstacle thrown in my direction, I remained focused on academics knowing it would be my golden ticket out of the projects. I graduated as Valedictorian from Garrett A. Morgan Elementary School and gave such a moving and enthusiastic speech that I became a hood celebrity.

In the midst of standing ovations, pictures with the Mayor and congratulatory hugs from complete strangers, I broke down in tears looking for Lynnette. Without her leading by example and showing me success was in my DNA, I certainly would not have pursued or pushed as hard. At that very moment, I made a mental note to always identify amazing leaders and mirror the very best in them. I was so moved by the audience's heartfelt reaction to my speech entitled, *"Excellence without Excuses"*, that I committed to coming back once a month to tutor underclassmen.

As a result of my academic excellence at Garrett A. Morgan, I received scholarship offers to attend some of the most prestigious prep schools in the nation. I had my choice of schools in Boston, upstate New York and Chicago. Although flattered by the prep schools' interest in me, my answer was a resounding, "No, thank you." I was needed in my hood and could not fathom being away from my family again.

PRINCIPLE #7 - FAMILY FIRST

Opportunities will come and go, but it's important that you stay true to who you are and what you value most. For me, it was family first.

Even though money was tight, Mom enrolled me in R.T. Hudson, a Seventh Day Adventist private school in the Bronx. While turning down academic scholarships of $20,000 a year, Mom was robbing Peter to pay a tuition she could not afford. This was a huge sacrifice for our family. We made ends meet by eating peanut butter and jelly sandwiches, powdered carnation milk and government cheese that didn't melt. Even though there always seemed to be more month than money, we survived. Prior to going to R.T. Hudson, I had decided I wanted to become a lawyer. At that time, I had no idea what lawyers did or what was required to become one. I just wanted to be a lawyer because, Michael, a guy at my church was a lawyer.

When I reached adulthood, I discovered that Michael wasn't actually a lawyer; he was a paralegal of some sort. However, the occupational variance didn't matter to me when I was a kid. All that mattered to me was he had a white Jaguar and was highly respected by members of the church—old and young alike. In my pursuit of the American Dream, I decided I would be like Mike. I started to put Esquire on my clothes and on the end of my name. I had no idea what it meant but it was a constant reminder that I had a goal that I needed to achieve. Goals and mentors are the most powerful tools in achieving any dream. Humans are creatures of imitation. We learn how to walk, talk, and achieve by observing those around us. A baby duck waddles when it walks because its mama waddles when she walks.

My glory years of high school were spent at Northeastern Academy, an absolutely fun and delightful place where I made dozens of lifelong friends. While school life was a blast, it seemed as though my home life was beginning to crumble again. Lynnette, my older sister, had graduated college and was living on her own. My brother, Eddie, was attending college in Alabama, and Evelyn got married and moved out of the house.

My family unit, my core had broken up. Although Denair and I were the best of friends things weren't the same in the house. While Mom remained my rock, it was difficult watching dad stagger into the house once every few weeks in a drunken stupor. He seemed to have no qualms about shouting profanities and blasting the TV at three o'clock in the morning on a school night. I guess in his condition he couldn't make a distinction between day or night, weekday or weekend. I was appalled by the nerve of him ordering Mom to cook him a meal hours before she had to get up and commute to work. His behavior was especially hard to swallow since we were on government assistance (food stamps) and he contributed absolutely nothing to the family financially. As a former New York City Police Officer who had made the cover of the largest newspaper in the country for his bravery and excellence, I suspect it was quite

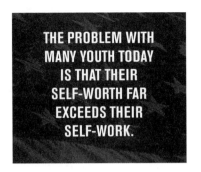

THE PROBLEM WITH MANY YOUTH TODAY IS THAT THEIR SELF-WORTH FAR EXCEEDS THEIR SELF-WORK.

humbling for him to walk the halls of buildings he'd once patrolled. It seemed he was progressively moving closer and closer to despondency.

Meanwhile, I had a full plate in high school as class president. I did everything imaginable (legal that is) to help Mom make ends meet. I was the original hustle man. I wasn't too proud to work any job because I wanted finer clothes, finer women, and I enjoyed eating quality food. The problem with many youth today is that their self-worth far exceeds their self-work.

PRINCIPLE # 8 - WORK = MONEY

Many feel they are above certain jobs or opportunities and would rather stay home than work menial jobs. There are a lot of prideful and broke people. I believe you should do what you got to do, so you can do what you want to do!

Having an appreciation for the Arts, I wrote poetry. To make a few extra dollars, I'd print out a few black and white copies of my pieces and place them in a gold frame. In no time at all I was moving units all over the Bronx, throughout Harlem and all points in between. I also had side gigs, one of which was delivering packages from the airport to downtown businesses with Mr. Wilson, a history teacher from my high school. We picked up parcels for Sureway Air Express, which was a bootleg version of FedEx. Their motto was, *"There's a right way, a wrong way, and a Sureway."* I had quite the hectic schedule. I worked from 8:00 p.m. until 2:00 a.m. then I'd rush home take a shower, have a brief nap, give my homework a quick once over, have worship with Mom at 5:00 a.m., and then I was off to school. While this grueling schedule would have broken most teenagers and adults, I embraced the hectic paced since it offered me the chance to (in the words of rapper, 50 Cent), get rich or die trying.

Although I had a decent amount of cash coming in during my sophomore year, I agreed to try my hand at rapping when a good friend, Roger Thomas, suggested we start our own rap duo. I thought, why not? I loved being in the spotlight, I had a great speaking voice, and rappers appeared to make a ton of money. Why not rock the ones and twos?

After meeting a few producers, we agreed to work with a crew who loved our sound so much they agreed to front the money for our studio time and demo. Word spread very quickly about our rap duo. People were excited to meet us and thought we would be the next big thing. Although LL Cool J was killing the game, many thought we had a smoother sound and style than the reigning king of New York City hip hop. Like Russell Simmons we'd build a rap empire.

We'd be the next big rappers coming out of The Bronx; KRS One, Melle Mel, Slick Ric, now us. Come to think of it, I'm not sure if we even had a name. Not a problem, the streets were talking. Our debut song, "Judgment Day", would be a hit. Before the final tracks were cut and our deal was inked, Mom caught wind of my desire to rap and put a halt to my promising musical career by ordering me to cease and desist the foolishness. Ever the enterprising one, I defied her orders. With the producers and my rap partner nudging me to complete our demo,

I spent an entire Friday evening recording in the studio. What was I doing recording tracks on the Sabbath? *'Mom is going to KILL me,'* I said. The ever-confident Roger said not to worry because he'd take care of it. Before I realized what was going on, Roger had picked up the phone, dialed my mother and announced that he was Sergeant Joe. In a muffled voice he told her the kids were fine and in his custody. He mentioned there was no need for her to come down to the precinct as they would be dropping me home after they finished processing their paperwork. Before kindly saying goodnight and ending the call, Mom asked good old Sgt. three basic questions:

1) His Badge Number
2) Precinct Identification
3) Incident Number

Boy, did Roger ever stammer and stutter. While he thought he did an amazing job, I knew I'd be dead once I got home. Having been married to a police officer for ten years, Mom knew the lingo and realized something was fishy. During my late night walk home, my mind raced back to a similar frigid walk I'd had nine years earlier. I told myself history wouldn't be repeating itself. No spanking tonight! As soon as Mom opened the door, I blurted out the truth! She sat me down and quietly explained that she was 100% certain it was Roger on the phone, and she had a pretty good idea I was fooling around with that rap thing on the Sabbath.

Before praying with me she told me she was prepared to whip me black and blue if I came into the house with that awful lie. While I was excited to escape the evening without a devastating beat down, the victory was bittersweet as I knew Roger and I had what it took to make it to the top of the rap chart. By all accounts the demo we cut that night was amazing. Years later as I watch my rap partner, Roger, perform on some of the world's largest stages including the Jay Leno Show, David Letterman, Carnegie Hall, etc. as the founder and lead rapper for Naturally 7, I could only wonder if I had missed my shot at living the American Dream.

With my musical career in the tank, I pivoted and followed Roger's lead into the fast food business. Roger was making a killing at a Queens Boulevard McDonald's in a seedy part of town. Roger was the acting crew chief responsible for making sure the lower employees stayed on task. After the McDonald's he was working at was robbed at gunpoint and the workers ushered into the walk-in freezer, Roger decided he would relocate to one of McDonald's finer establishments in downtown Manhattan. He invited me to apply for a crew chief position while he applied for an assistant manager gig at the 59th Street store next door to Bloomingdale's. This was a triple A McDonald's. There was a noticeable difference in the cleanliness standards, food quality, and employee to customer attitudes. I had never worked for McDonald's or any fast food company for that matter. Roger told me not to worry; he said I should just do what he did. Roger made the cut as assistant manager and I was hired as a crew chief with absolutely no experience on my first day. We were the dynamic duo once again. I watched Roger prepare burgers, fish sandwiches, fries, and apple pies. Whatever he did, I did. It was like playing a high stakes game of follow the leader.

PRINCIPLE # 9
MAKE YOUR WORK, WORK FOR YOU

You should give your all to whatever job you have. In doing so, you'll naturally gain leverage, and benefit far more than just getting a paycheck. Your work will begin to work for you.

Roger and I took on the most difficult tasks at our store. We became kings of the burgers and embraced collecting and taking out the trash. We became so efficient that we were able to handle the lunch time crowd alone. We became so good at mastering the tasks no one else wanted to do, that we were able to control our own destiny. We were so beloved that we were allowed to take a 3-hour uninterrupted paid break in the employee lounge in appreciation for us doing all the grunt work in the restaurant. The coup de grace or icing on the cake was working the night shift and having the ability to take home leftovers rather than chucking them in the trash at the end of the night. We were able to make a nice little mint selling leftover burgers and fries to hungry commuters who gladly appreciated the lower prices and delivery service.

As the weather got colder and the Christmas season approached, Roger and I moved our quest for the American Dream indoors. We were hired as commission-based salesmen for an aggressive electronics chain known as The Wiz. The Wiz, whose slogan was, _Nobody Beats the Wiz,_ was battling the market leader in N.Y., which was an electronics chain called, Crazy Eddie. Crazy Eddie's motto was that his prices were so low they were I-N-S-A-A-A-N-E! Our timing and positioning couldn't have been better. Our store was highly incentivized for us to always beat the competition. We mastered the sales game by knowing which products had the highest commission. Every customer was also urged to get an extended warranty for which we received bonuses based on warranty sales. The man who learned the commission game could sell less, work fewer hours and still take home double or triple what the average guy did. Mastering the profit system in any business is the key to winning and winning big. Who knew selling televisions, walkmans, and radios could be so lucrative. Three months after the holidays, when I was no longer working for the Wiz, checks were still flowing in. I eventually turned my older brother and his college roommate on to that opportunity.

When the holiday season ended, I refocused my time and energy back on school work and my duties as student body president. During my senior year, I established a strong bond with my chemistry teacher, Melcher Monk. From the first time I met him in the eleventh grade, I admired his character and morality. His voice was as deep as the ocean and powerful enough to silence the class with a single greeting; "Good Morning." He loved his job and often went beyond the call of duty, as he frequently invited those students who did well to his home for dinner.

The way he dressed said much about his lifestyle. When I came into classroom B-3 on the first day of school and saw a teacher in an outfit that looked as though it costs over $400, I was impressed. In actuality, I found out that he was also a professional tailor. He could mold and create the most elegant wedding dress in the blink of an eye. Mr. Monk, ever the teacher, taught me the finer points of sewing. Within a matter of months, I was earning thousands of dollars designing choir robes for churches from Baltimore to Boston.

PRINCIPLE # 10 - ADOPT A MENTOR

Most mentors will choose you and take you under their wing. There's also value in adopting your own mentor. Look for someone who's different so they can challenge you on different levels.

Mr. Monk became more than just a distant star, he became my sunlamp. I looked up to him for so many different reasons. He was like a father and friend to me. I hated my own father who was seldom around and, even when he was, he reeked of the streets and alcohol. All my real father offered me was sorrow and misery. I kept my feelings bottled up deep inside. One day while at Mr. Monk's tailor shop, I began to cry. I could no longer contain my sorrow. My tears cascaded down my cheeks and onto his $700 sewing machine. He turned and kindly looked at me, then he said; *"You're going to make it rust."* He had a way of cheering me up and brightening my mood with his humor. I remember a time he asked me to pass out some papers in class. Just as I was getting to the last person on the second row, he hit me with the Delta Paddle. Pow!! The paddle was about the size and weight of a cricket bat. His ability to chuckle and grin when the world had climbed upon his shoulders was his greatest asset. Whenever he told a good joke or made fun of someone in the class, his laugh-lines made his face raisin-like. He had many lighthearted expressions, one of which was; *"You haven't failed until you've tried."*

In the two years that I knew him, he became my father, my brother, and my friend. He taught me how to just appreciate my father for who he was. I will never forget all the things I learned from him. He opened my mind and my understanding of many things. When I needed a role model the most, he stepped in. He was my hero.

> **I GAVE MY SPEECH WHILE SHARING THE STAGE WITH THE KEYNOTE SPEAKER, RENOWNED NEUROSURGEON, DR. BEN CARSON.**

After spending my junior and senior high school years shadowing Mr. Monk, I felt as though I could conquer the world. Thanks to Mr. Monk's support, I graduated as Salutatorian and delivered a stirring speech about reaching for your dreams. I gave my speech while sharing the stage with the keynote speaker, renowned neurosurgeon, Dr. Ben Carson.

Many were amazed at my ability to juggle academics, economics, and an unbalanced home-life. I had resolved to be fearless and relentless in my pursuit of the American Dream. I wanted to leave a legacy for my family, classmates, and my hood.

CHAPTER 4

"COLLEGE BOUND"

About three o'clock one morning, my friends Kenny, Melcher Monk and I were racing down Virginia's Interstate 95 doing about 101 miles per hour. We were stopped by a burly State Trooper whose siren was blaring so loud I was afraid to stick my head up from the back seat. The officer turned on the brightest high-beams I've ever seen. He must have been every bit of 6 foot 6 inches tall. He looked like Goliath as he approached our vehicle. We were in a two-week-old sports car with tinted windows, and I feared the officer might assume the car was stolen. I didn't know if the temporary tag on Kenny's car was even legitimate. I thought to myself, I should have taken a plane and avoided the back seat of that car all together. Things were definitely not looking good. *"What seems to be the…"* was all Kenny was able to say before the beefy trooper with a bad attitude shouted, *"License and registration"*, over and over again. As Kenny reached toward his right back pocket to get his wallet, the officer flinched and made a sudden move toward his gun. I shut my eyes and prepared for the worst. Kenny carefully extended his wallet and out popped his driver's license along with his gold Maryland police badge.

With this revelation, the situation de-escalated quickly to a less than life threatening tone. The trooper, still a little on edge, then asked Kenny, *"Where's the fire? What's*

FOR A POOR KID FROM THE SOUTH BRONX, IT WAS THE MOST AMAZING PLACE I'D EVER LAID EYES ON.

the rush?" Kenny calmly told Officer Grumpy that he was rushing to get me to Alabama so I wouldn't miss my first day of college in the morning. Disaster averted. From the time I was seven years old, I'd dreamed of escaping New York, furthering my education and becoming a successful attorney. College was my ticket to greatness and that night on the Interstate, my entire life flashed before my eyes. I thanked the Lord for His mercy and told Kenny to slow down. I'd worked too hard my entire life for this opportunity. I couldn't have my shot at success ruined. If necessary, I was prepared to walk through the night and the next night in order to make it to campus without any further incidents. Nine hours later I was driving thru the gates of Oakwood College. For a poor kid from the South Bronx, it was the most amazing place I'd ever laid eyes on. The grass was green, flowers were blooming, there was no graffiti on the wall and people actually smiled and waved when you looked in their direction. I had to pinch myself repeatedly. This was definitely the place I'd plant my flag.

My first six days on the Oakwood campus was everything I imagined and more. The girls were prettier than expected, the buffet-style cafeteria allowed me to eat to my heart's content, and the curriculum was challenging.

On day seven, while I was standing in the lobby of the freshman girl's dormitory chatting it up with a few potential lady friends, my brother (who was a senior), and his roommate crept up behind me and pulled my sweatpants all the way down to my ankles. All my cool points were gone. Welcome to college.

After recovering from the most embarrassing episode in my life, I got a job as a roofer and established a tight bond with a small group of freshmen guys who were just as focused and competitive as I. Game on!

By my ninth day on campus, I quickly went into grind mode, making alliances with popular kids from large cities like New York, Chicago, Atlanta & Los Angeles. I decided I would be elected student body president by the end of my sophomore year. This preemptive move wasn't about striking while the irons were hot, it was more about eliminating my competition before they knew they were even in the game. Being student body president was a natural extension of previous leadership positions I'd held in elementary, middle and high school.

I always had a desire to challenge my self-worth against the best competition I could find. Could a poor kid from the Bronx compete with these kids who were the third and fourth generation offspring of doctors, lawyers, and preachers? In the back of my mind, I was always thinking, *"Could any good thing come from the Bronx?"* My answer was always, *"Yes."* And I'll prove it. If Jesus could come from lowly and obscure Bethlehem, then something worthwhile would emerge from my patchwork upbringing.

Since the presidential election wasn't for another twenty months, I decided a great way to build my brand and solidify political connections was to run for the vacant student body senate seat reserved for freshmen. I immediately went to work befriending everyone on campus. As a disciple of the great Dale Carnegie, I knew the value of winning friends and influencing people. I almost felt guilty running for office against my competitors. Although they had pedigree, influence and deeper pockets (mine were empty), I would be victorious using people power.

PRINCIPLE # 11 - PEOPLE POWER

There is no force stronger than connecting and relating to people. Building relationships with people is a powerful tool, when looking for a role of power, leadership or influence.

I was heavily involved in intermural sports and the black history bowl (a trivia competition about black history). I got a second job on campus and was involved in the nightly religious campfire-type programs they held on campus. I even joined the drama club and choir. I used every opportunity to be diverse and connect with every facet of campus life. I considered myself a campus Leonardo Da Vinci, the Renaissance man. I wanted to experience every aspect of college life. I loved it. I embraced it. I decided it.

Ever the entrepreneur, I spent a great deal of time loading up on chips, sodas, bread, and packages of ramen noodles from the local grocery store that I'd retail to kids burning the midnight oil. I'd become Wal-Mart Central. I would charge them just enough for me to make a profit but not so much that they'd decide to go purchase the items elsewhere. This was a dicey balancing act; if I overcharged, the pain would outweigh the gain.

My other hustle was cutting hair. I was a self-proclaimed master barber with my Oyster barber set. Every Friday afternoon like clockwork, the entire campus would clean their dorm rooms for inspection by the resident assistants and get coiffured for the weekend. For the ladies this included perms and last minute runs to the mall for stockings and miscellaneous finery. For the guys who'd be out on the prowl, a haircut was a necessary expense.

I faced a challenge in my wing of the dorm—there were at least twenty self-proclaimed master barbers who charged anywhere from $5.00 to $10.00 for a cut. I needed to secure some steady clientele so I approached this mission with the calculated effort of a drug dealer trying to take over a corner. I discounted my prices, gave away free cuts to first timers, and changed times and locations to one-up on the competition. It wasn't unusual for me to go to the customer's room to cut their hair. There were benefits to offering convenience to the client. Being mobile gave me a real advantage; I was able to charge a little more than my competitors and still maintained my customer loyalty. I even went as far as to give customers a free hair cut on every fifth visit. My boys used to think this was ludicrous, but it was my version of a customer loyalty program.

Many of my friends marveled at the fact that I was very social—attended every campus event, and still managed to ace all my exams and graduate with a 3.95 GPA. My secret was simple; early on in life I learned the value of prioritizing, goal setting, and sacrificing. I knew if I wanted more out of life I had to be willing to give more. I knew more than half of the student body by name and another 25% by face. Names have never been my strong suit. I think Facebook was made for people like me. To make up for my inability to remember people's names, I came up with substitutes like, *"Hey, Sis"*, *"What's up, bro"*, *"Good to see you, doctor"*, and other similar expressions. I wasn't going to let my inability to readily recall names keep me from connecting with the student body. My second year of college began with a slight distraction, as my girlfriend of five years enrolled at my college. Our relationship was solid while long distance, but in person it became one more thing I had to juggle while campaigning for student body president. There were promises of better student housing, lower tuition, and cries of *power to the people* at my rallies.

PRINCIPLE # 12 - POWER OF THE TEAM

There's power in connecting and uniting with other people who share your vision, opinion or beliefs. When fighting for a cause or building a movement, surround yourself with people of passion who will persevere despite adversity.

There was talk of election rigging and violence at the polls. At the end of the day, I hitched my political wagon to a very radical student on campus who was also running for student body president. The local think tank on campus suggested we merge our campaign as our platforms closely mirrored one another. The think tank was correct. My running mate and I carried the day. The school year ended with us planning a massive mind blowing program on the scale of FDR's new deal.

When school re-opened after summer break, there were whisperings of a scandal everywhere on campus. The word was out that my comrade and co-president was a soon-to-be father. And the soon-to-be mother was also on campus. TMZ would have had a field day for the first two months of school. With the rumors confirmed and reputations shattered, the newly elected president was expelled from school. Our political enemies felt vindicated and I was ushered in to take the helm. It was my duty to restore order, trust, and stick to the big initiatives.

Despite the best laid plans, life happens. I replaced some administrative staff in our student government that had been appointed by my former colleague. The people replaced were not happy and vowed to ruin my administration by joining ranks with my former political opponents. Who had time for school? I was combating confessed enemies and former insiders. TMZ could have come back again for a second round of allegations and mudslinging. Just when I thought things couldn't get any worse, I received a call that shook me to my core. Reese, my favorite cousin, the guy who shared his bed, food and clothes with me when I was homeless, died after being shot ten times at point blank range.

I hastily left school to be near my family during this trying period. A would-be tough guy, Reese headed a crew of twenty thugs and drug dealers. At the age of twenty, he was making a few thousand dollars a week. He was a ghetto hero in Melrose Projects. Reese often talked about leaving the fast money and being a successful businessman. We agreed that our children would grow up together and we would live down the street from each other in our mansions. The dream never happened; the streets claimed him and took his life. He left a newborn, multiple girlfriends, and family members in mourning. We were both strong, powerful leaders. He chose the street life and I chose college. With his wit, charm and innate leadership ability he could easily have run a successful legitimate business.

His funeral had me so distraught and upset that after the funeral I got lost on my way driving to the cemetery. I had lived in that city my entire life and knew it like the back of my hand. The fact that I got lost was a sure sign that my stress cup was full. I arrived at the cemetery in New Jersey almost an hour after everyone else. I just couldn't focus and I couldn't get the sight of my favorite cousin whom I shared every waking moment with as kids, now riddled with bullets out of my mind. I started to have nightmares and spit blood from episodes of chewing my tongue while I was sleeping. This had never happened to me before. It was the first time someone close to me died. I returned to school in a mental fog. The first couple of weeks were grim. I was battered from every

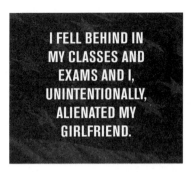

> I FELL BEHIND IN MY CLASSES AND EXAMS AND I, UNINTENTIONALLY, ALIENATED MY GIRLFRIEND.

direction. My political enemies and fired staff members joined forces against me. I fell behind in my classes and exams and I, unintentionally, alienated my girlfriend. I needed a break but there was no break in sight. Life offers challenges to fit whatever size you are. I had always been a firm believer that the Almighty doesn't give you more than you can bear. Where was the Lord when I needed Him most? I wanted to stay in my room and avoid everyone. My empire was collapsing and taking me with it.

Most of the student body was not aware of my life challenges and just assumed that I had shrunk and retreated from the current school social scene. Eventually, I recovered and finished the year strong. Although, my legacy was subpar from the pax romana I had envisioned, I finished Oakwood with a 3.95 GPA.

After graduation, I began to study for the Law School Admissions Test (LSAT). However, due to lingering personal issues, I failed to give my LSAT studies the time it deserved. To be frank, my studying for the exam was mediocre at best. I knew a few students who got into law school and they claimed the exam wasn't that hard. I was doing well on my practice exams in non-test like conditions and thought I was ready. I took the exam that fall and got what I deserved, a score in the bottom twenty-percentile. I went into panic mode.

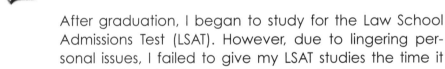

PRINCIPLE # 13 - FINISH STRONG

It's important to put forth your best efforts in life, but it's just as important to finish what you start. It's not enough to finish, you have to finish strong! True Success is found in those who never quit. Push with a sense of urgency and finish strong.

I must admit, I was utterly disappointed. It seemed all of my academic accolades were for nothing. I wondered if I'd ever become a lawyer. My chances at a scholarship were gone. My mother would never be able to pay for me to go to law school. What school would want me anyway? There was not enough student loan money being offered to make law school a possibility unless it accompanied a full or partial scholarship. There was no one to turn to; no friends, no family, no fairy godmother or white knight. Would I just become another statistic? So sorry, Mom. Now what?

I left school and moved back in with Mom—back into the projects. I was so embarrassed and felt defeated. I got a job being a substitute teacher at my former high school thanks to Mr. Monk. I was on call every day on an as-needed basis. It sucked! All my hopes of doing something bigger in life were fading fast. I felt angry and powerless.

When the school's history teacher died I was offered a full time position. I was familiar with the students and I had always aced that subject. I was barely twenty years old and some of the seniors were already eighteen and nineteen years old. Some days I felt more like a peer than a teacher while working at the school. While I recognized teaching was an honorable profession, it wasn't where I wanted to stake my flag. When summer break came, I took a job as a summer camp assistant director. I took my LSAT study books with me to the summer retreat and thought I would be able to study between camp activities. No such luck, the camp regime was so aggressive by the time I finished soccer, swimming, horseback riding, math classes, bowling, archery, laundry, three meals, and two snacks a day, I was exhausted. The summer was slipping away and I was not prepared to take the LSAT a second time. I was watching my dream crumble before my eyes. One day during camp activities, I was called to the director's office over the loud speaker. When I arrived, I was notified that my college roommate of two years had just been killed in a motorcycle accident. NOOOOOOOOO!!!!! I couldn't take anymore. What on earth was going on? Was I being targeted by God as part of some cosmic experiment to test my pain threshold? Was I to be Job 2.0? I give up, I quit. God, You win.

This was the second funeral that I attended for someone I loved within a matter of months. The casket was open and my roommate had a hat on because his skull was crushed by the impact of the fall. I broke down in gut-wrenching tears during the funeral. The last of my will to win was taken. I went from bursting with excitement about taking on life to throwing up my hands and waving the white flag.

After summer camp was over, I went back to the Bronx and had a host of odd jobs. For twelve months or more I was the prodigal son wallowing in pig slop. I was born for more; born to win, what the hell was happening? My dreams turned to nightmares and I went from being a driver to being a passenger on my life's road. I read, "Why Should White Guys Have All the Fun", a book about Reginald Lewis, a black lawyer who owned a $4-billion company. Reading this book and a second book called, "The Financier, the autobiography of Andre

Meyer", shook me out of my pity party stupor. Reading was always my greatest motivator, and at a time I needed it most, these stories of men who didn't quit reignited my fire.

CHAPTER 5

"THE COME BACK!"

"Make failure your teacher, not your undertaker."
- Zig Ziglar

I was born to win; I'd never known defeat. I was the Iron Mike Tyson of the classroom. I was crushing it on the speaking circuit; scoring checks totaling $3,000 a day. I was also authoring children's encyclopedias. At age twenty, I had an aura of invincibility and indestructibility. The Law School Admission Test would be just another in a long line of swift decisive victories. But like Iron Mike, I didn't fully respect my opponent; I wasn't all in. I had a so-so commitment. I didn't give it my all. The world was my platform, and on the biggest stage of my life, I suddenly fell flat on my face. I was knocked down but I wasn't out. I came back into the ring with purpose and determination. I knew success had a price and I was willing to pay it this time around. Every second of every day I was resolved to give nothing less than 1000%. I left nothing to chance; every move I made was intentional.

Above my bed was a poem that read as follows:

"Excellence is never an accident; it is the result of high intention, sincere effort, intelligent direction, skillful execution and the vision to see obstacles as opportunities."
~ Anonymous

THERE ARE MANY SHORTCUTS TO FAILURE, BUT THERE ARE NO SHORTCUTS TO TRUE SUCCESS.

Six months prior to my second dance with the LSAT, I recaptured my MOJO by teaching poor and disadvantaged students from the Bronx advanced test-taking techniques for their college entrance exam. After bombing on the LSAT, I may not have been the ideal person to teach these students critical thinking and proficiency. It appeared God had a sense of humor. Since I had scored in the top one-percent nationally on both the ACT and SAT, as a high school student, I was given carte blanche in creating a course that would elevate their chances of getting into top tier universities across the country.

On the first day of the course, I repeated the profound words of Orrin Woodward: *"There are many shortcuts to failure, but there are no shortcuts to true success."*

Day in and day out, I asked my students what price they were willing to pay. I told them they had to be willing to give up some things to achieve greatness. Would it be TV? Would it be basketball? Would it be a boyfriend or girlfriend? I told them they would have to become uncomfortable to become comfortable.

The six weeks I spent with the underprivileged kids were priceless. I had become more focused and inspired than at any other time in my life. I was literally on fire after the course ended. I took my gloves off and came out swinging. I would hold myself accountable and follow the same principles I preached to the kids.

I was encouraged by John Wesley who said, *"Light yourself on fire with passion and people will come from miles to watch you burn."*

I was excited about my upcoming LSAT, and it was evident in the way I walked, the pitch of my voice and my level of focus.

PRINCIPLE # 14 - LASER FOCUS

There will be times in your life when you have to have a laser focus. In those times, it's important to put all of your attention, energy, and focus into reaching one goal.

With 3000 hours remaining before the exam, I implemented a regimen that would please a drill sergeant.

- I enrolled in a Kaplan LSAT prep class in Lower Manhattan, and had to commute three-hours per day.

- I doubled my test preparation time from four weeks prior to the exam to eight weeks.

- I began studying fifteen to sixteen hours a day, six days a week, rather than the two to three hours I'd done for the first LSAT.

- I went from taking five practice tests to taking 100 practice tests.

- I happily went from answering fifty questions a day to answering 1,500 a day.

A well-to-do young lady, whom I briefly dated, called to tell me her dad would offer me a six-figure salary if I gave up this law school thing and moved with her overseas to run his export business. I was fully committed and quitting

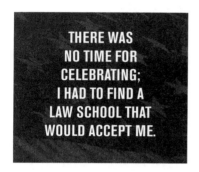

THERE WAS NO TIME FOR CELEBRATING; I HAD TO FIND A LAW SCHOOL THAT WOULD ACCEPT ME.

was not an option. I quickly decided that everything not related to me obliterating the LSAT would have to be put on hold. My eyes were on the prize; I was on my way to Harvard and no distractions were allowed.

For the next 2,500 hours I put all my moneymaking hustles to the side. My speaking gigs were canceled, I didn't go on dates, and calls from lady friends went unanswered. Mom's small two-bedroom apartment was converted into a makeshift law library in the projects.

On the day of the LSAT exam, I was filled with a sense of calm. I bowed my head and thanked The Lord for His mercy and for this second chance. I was astonished when I finished the exam more than an hour early, and assumed that I had either aced it or completely bombed. There was no room for anything in between. The exam could only be taken three times, and I did not want to get down to my last strike.

I was on pins and needles the next four weeks waiting for my scores. The day my scores arrived, I was a nervous wreck. After peeking into the envelope I was absolutely floored; I scored 170! The highest possible score was 180. My come back had been complete! Had anyone ever scored in the bottom 20% and then catapulted themselves into the top one-percent in less than a year? I wept for hours. The weight of the world had been lifted off my shoulders. I could finally exhale. I was at peace for all of 24-hours. There was no time for celebrating; I had to find a law school that would accept me.

With a 170 LSAT score, a 3.95 grade point average, and

ten years of leadership and community service, I should have been able to attend any law school in the nation. I dreamed of going to Harvard but I didn't apply because the application fees were more than $150. Each school had an application fee, and my confidence was so shattered from my first LSAT that I never imagined doing well enough to make it into Harvard. I had to be strategic with my limited cash so I didn't want to risk losing $150 if my application was rejected. I did spend the money to apply to 10 other schools, and received a full scholarship to each. The most prestigious of the law schools were Boston University and Northwestern University which both ranked among the top ten law schools.

With several schools beginning to push for my response, I was starting to feel a bit overwhelmed. Mom told me to pray over it, believing my choice of school would really affect my career. Late one night I fell asleep watching television, my eyes opened to a story of the civil rights movement and the great accomplishments of Thurgood Marshall.

Thurgood Marshall was a great lawyer who broke Jim Crow era laws that made life all but unbearable for African Americans. Marshall challenged head-on the legal underpinning of racial segregation, with his greatest victory being Brown V. The Board of Education which undid the doctrine of "separate but equal" established by the 1896 Supreme Court case *Plessy v. Ferguson.*

In 1965 President Lyndon Johnson, appointed Thurgood Marshall U.S. Solicitor General, the federal government's attorney before the Supreme Court. In 1967, Thurgood Marshall became the first African American appointed to the Supreme Court. Imagine my surprise, when I learned he was a graduate of Howard University School of Law. If Howard University could produce one Supreme Court

I NEVER LET MONEY STOP ME FROM REALIZING MY DREAMS.

Justice, then surely it could produce another. Although flattered by the courtship of the top tier law schools, I made up my mind that I would follow in Justice Marshall's footsteps and attend Howard University School of Law.

Within thirty-six hours of deciding to move to the nation's capital and attend Howard University, I received a notice that I had been accepted into a mentorship program for aspiring black lawyers. I hadn't informed Howard University of my decision, nor did I recall applying for the program, but I was grateful for the invitation. When I received notice of the program, the letter stated that the program would begin in two days. This was a complete reversal of fortune. I was happy and excited to be invited to the program but I didn't have any money to attend. My mother, siblings, and I were flat broke after using most of our discretionary income applying to various law schools. I never let money stop me from realizing my dreams.

So, I packed a duffle bag, gathered up $150, and kissed my mom goodbye. My mother was worried and concerned as most mothers would be. She asked questions like, "Where are you going to stay? How are you going to eat?" I didn't care about any of those things. I was focused on the fact that I'd been given a second shot at my dreams, and I was not going to blow my (WOO) Window of Opportunity a second time.

PRINCIPLE # 15 - FAITH THAT MOVES

Many times people claim to have faith, but they're held captive by their fears. Real faith doesn't always make sense, and will move you to action regardless of your financial situation.

Within forty-eight hours of the letter's arrival, I was on the Greyhound bus from New York to Washington D.C. I was truly going on faith. The bus ticket was about $25, which meant that all the money I had left in the world was about $120. My mother and brother worked to try to secure housing for me with various family members I had never met. My mother called some professor who was a distant relative and asked if I could stay at his house during my internship. He kindly turned us down stating that he was newly re-married and didn't think his new bride would approve. My brother had better luck and secured a sofa for me to sleep on at his former college roommate's house in the D.C. area. To be honest, I was prepared to sleep in the park if it came down to it. I arrived at the internship on time and met some of the brightest and best minds in the country. We were as-signed mentors at two Fortune 100 law firms in D.C. I shadowed top-rated attorneys every day. I drafted briefs, letters, learned the law, and did research.

I found a job working at Equifax in Tysons Corner, Virginia, a day after my program began. My brother's friend let me stay at his place but he wouldn't give me a key for some reason. That was becoming quite a pain because of the crazy hours I was keeping with the internship and the new job. There were a few nights I found myself locked out.

Eventually, I relocated to a distant cousin's house. There

was some tension in that situation because I didn't have a car and my cousin lived far from any public transportation. I was not prepared to risk my job and internship because of transportation problems. It was still the middle of summer and the weather was nice. Most days, I transported my things in my big duffle bag. I looked like a veteran returning from war or a homeless vagabond. I just felt better keeping all of my stuff close in the event somebody kicked me out. I spent about a week living with some girls in the internship program. Then, I spent about two or three nights sleeping outdoors with one eye open at a park near DuPont Circle. My life was becoming sheer and utter madness. I started getting to my internship at the law firm hours early just so I could get cleaned up in the restroom and look human. I felt like life was testing me.

Eventually, a girl in my internship program told me about a hostel where I could stay for $13 a night. I guess the wear and tear of living everywhere and on the street was starting to show, or maybe she surmised that my living conditions were suspect because I was always toting a sixty-pound duffle bag with me wherever I went. The hostel was in the downtown D.C. area. It's like a hotel where you share a room with about twenty people. It was clean and cheap. They had lockers for $2 a day. Everyone was required to leave each day and completely take all of their belongings. It was not like a homeless shelter it was a dormitory for travelers from other countries. There were two restrooms for the fifty or so occupants. It worked great unless you arrived to the hostel late and there were no beds left.

I had other options; the park always had vacancies. If necessary, I could crash there on a moment's notice. One night some kids from the internship had a party to celebrate the end of the internship and beginning of law

I WAS GOING TO BE THE NEXT THURGOOD MARSHALL.

school. My duffle bag and I attended the party, and I ended up falling asleep there on the sofa from sheer exhaustion. The house where the party was held was owned by one of my friends from the program, and he allowed me to sleep through the night. To say I was grateful was an understatement. I ended up staying there a week or more after the party. The money I made from my job in Virginia was being spent on the little food I was eating and transportation costs. I managed to save $500 and, right before school started, I bought a Plymouth Reliant K car. It was blue, it was ugly, but it was mine. I looked like a security guard in that car.

Once law school started, I was all the way zoned in. Nothing else mattered. My first class on day one started with some teacher talking about look to your left and look to your right and by next year one or two of you will not be back. So, I looked to my left and looked to my right and thought, sayonara to those two, because I was going to be the next Thurgood Marshall.

I did well my first year of law school and eventually found a place to rent. My grandmother gave me the money for the initial rent deposit and used her good credit to help me secure the lease. However, with the costs of school being so high even with a full scholarship, I couldn't afford the rent by year two of law school. So, over the summer, I moved in with my, then, girlfriend and thought I could balance love and law like the scales of justice. Love took up way too much time and I decided I had to move out if I would have any chance of staying the course. On the day I was moving out, I ran into an older gentleman next door who asked me if I was a law student. I responded, *"Yes, I am."* He said, *"I have a place you can live for $500 a month."* Talk about perfect timing...God was looking out for me. When I was leaving my girlfriend's house I really had nowhere to go. My new place was literally a few feet away from where I'd just moved from. While I was still close to my girlfriend's house and mildly distracted, I could at least shut the door and be the master of my domain.

I was grateful for the roof over my head but there was a catch to the old man's offer. He regularly dropped off tons of legal papers that he wanted me to review, and requested that I draft legal filings on his behalf. I was feeling like Rumpelstiltskin. I was in a catch-22 situation. I desperately needed a place to live but this guy was working the stew out of me. Some days, I was ducking him and the girlfriend just to find a minute of peace. The upside of being his personal legal flunky was I got to work on many complex cases against some of the best lawyers in the country. I was gaining more real world legal practice than most of my class would see for another five to six years after leaving law school. We had one case against a major commercial bank that failed to record a deed in a timely manner, and in the interim the house was refinanced by a third party. I successfully maneuvered reassignment of the deed and defeated the bank's high priced legal team from my basement law firm. I was on a roll and probably won about six or more cases for my landlord that year. As I saw the value of my predicament, I started to embrace the experience and my stats like a basketball team evaluating their win-loss record.

Back at school, I was getting additional experience in a clinical program where I took criminal, divorce, and landlord/tenant cases as part of a program called Law

I WAS TOLD THAT MY MOTHER WAS STABBED ABOUT FORTY OR MORE TIMES AT HER HOME IN THE BRONX.

Students in Court. I had a total of twelve cases for the school year and won or successfully pled out every one of them. The next step was what really gave me the long term confidence to handle many future legal contests. I competed for and won the right to represent my school on a mock trial team. Our team was one of the best in the country and went to the national competition in Texas. In addition to bragging rights on the line, there was a pot of gold waiting for those students who proved to be all-stars. In the same manner NBA scouts went to the NCAA Final Four Tournament seeking the best and brightest players, many of the country's top legal firms sent representatives to the competitions to recruit top tier talent.

In a surprising upset, Howard University wiped the floor with the more prestigious Ivy League and top tier law schools in the country. Howard University Law School was back on the map and I was a major part of its rebirth.

Over the summer, I clerked for a District of Columbia Judge, and for a Federal Judge once school restarted. I had the ability to review cases of major importance and draft responses on behalf of my judges. My legal muscles were strong and I went into my final year of law school ready to hit the ground running. My belief in Howard was justified. I was on the verge of living my dream.

Just as school was getting started, I got a desperate and urgent call from one of my siblings informing me that my mother was in the hospital emergency room. When I asked what happened, I was told that my mother was stabbed about forty or more times at her home in the

MY FOCUS AND WILL TO WIN WAS BLUNTED BY MY CONCERN FOR MY MOTHER.

Bronx. I asked a thousand questions, *"Who did it? Was she robbed? Did they catch the guy?"* I'd had my share of death and I was scared to ask the biggest question, *"Will she make it?"* I packed up my K car and took off to New York within an hour of getting the call. All of my siblings came from all over the country to be by my mother's bedside. My mother looked awful. She was swollen, bruised, bleeding, but thank God she was still here. I eventually got all the facts about what happened and I was very angry. I now understand how people can be filled with enough rage to kill and not care about the consequences.

My mother was stabbed in her head, back and arms with an icepick by a guy on parole. My mother was part of the prison ministries program at her church, and for the last thirty years or more visited the prisons to give Bible studies to inmates. The monster who tried to kill my mother was one of the Bible study inmates who was paroled, then baptized at my mother's church. After the baptism, there was a lunch at my mother's house. Once all the other guests left, the monster snapped. He later told the judge at his trial that the—*devil told him to kill her.* Thankfully, he was captured and sentenced to complete his original sentence plus additional time for attempted murder of my mother. The stabbing was more than twenty years ago, but my mother still has not fully recovered physically or emotionally. She has endured many surgeries, hospital visits, and counseling sessions. When my mother got out of the hospital, we relocated her out the Bronx. The attack on her caused me to sever my ties to the city of my youth.

The situation with my mother's attack took my 3-year law school wind away. My focus and will to win was blunted by my concern for my mother. Nursing her back to health and providing the assurance that we were there for her was more important than my degree. My teachers were very understanding, but I was losing my killer instinct for the law. Even if it wasn't lost entirely, I still felt like my sharp edge had become a dull blade. I stopped asking, *what's next?* because there was always another storm waiting to throw me for a loop.

During my final year of law school, I met my wife, Melodie. Things were beginning to look bright again. I saw her at church a few times but never thought anything would come of it. She was the hottest usher I'd ever seen. Anytime she was passing around the plate, I emptied my pockets. Cute girls collecting the offering—great strategy to get the tithes and offerings up.

After following the same strategy I used to ace my LSAT, I took the bar exam in July and scored in the top five-percent in Maryland. I had done so well on my Maryland Bar exam that I was eligible for a waiver into the Washington D.C. Bar. It's not easy to score high enough to get the waiver so I'm grateful that I aced the exam.

PRINCIPLE #16 - KNOW YOUR WORTH

Many people would love to work for the top companies in the world, but how many have the heart to work for themselves? When you know your worth you'll learn to take more risks and invest in yourself. Go get what you're worth.

After discovering that nearly one-third of Americans in

the workforce are dissatisfied with their jobs, I decided to open my own law firm. Why not? I had already defeated dozens of top lawyers while working from my bedroom, thanks to Mr. Rumpelstiltskin

My life-long dream of being an entrepreneur and running my own successful law practice was finally taking shape.

"As long as I am breathing, in my eyes, I am just beginning."
~ Criss Jami

CHAPTER 6

"THAT'S ENTERTAINMENT!"

It was a scorching summer day and I was backstage mingling with Lil Wayne, Busta Rhymes, and Luda. Was that Eve and Gwen Stefani going on stage?

I was beyond excited. Eve and Gwen Stefani were giving the performance of their lives singing Eve's chart-topping single, *"Let Me Blow Your Mind"*, at BET's 2001 Spring Bling Beach Party. As I chatted with Eve backstage after her performance, I realized she was more beautiful than I'd imagined. I had to pull it together quickly because there was a crisis brewing. The mayor of Daytona Beach was threatening to pull the plug on the entire weekend. There were thirty more big name Hip Hop artists like, Ja Rule, Lil John, & Snoop Dogg scheduled to hit the stage over the next three days.

If the show was canceled, BET would lose millions of dollars and a great deal of credibility. There were close to 50,000 college students converging on Daytona Beach hoping to be a part of our audience. Only the sexiest people gained access. The event was being filmed and would replay the entire summer. It was always one of our highest rated shows.

After arriving on the scene, I greeted the mayor and asked how I could be of service. He said, *"If I hear one more curse word today, I am going to shut the entire event down."* No one knew for sure if he had that kind of power or not, but we weren't going to test him and take chances with a million dollar live production going on. I told the current performer that we were in jeopardy of being shut down if he didn't curb his profanity. Just as I returned to assure the mayor that things were being re-solved, the artist in question, rapper Eminem, launched into a curse-laden chorus. All hell broke loose.

The mayor called in the police chief and the city attor-ney to shut the event down. As BET's head legal repre-sentative on location, I was not going to let the mayor shut us down. I went into Thurgood Marshall mode and pulled contracts, city codes, contract law, and any oth-er precedent I could rely on to keep the show going. After I had convinced the mayor that BET would bury him and the City of Daytona Beach in lawsuits for damages for the next ten years to compensate us for lost earnings, the mayor and his team chose to see things my way.

For an aspiring rapper turned corporate attorney, I was living the life of Riley. It was my dream job.

There were a few close calls with rappers who wanted to be gangsters at Spring Bling. One such confrontational incident happened when I told a rapper *"No, you can't come in. I never heard of you. If you want to get into the venue you and your entourage can wait in the line."* He looked tough with his crew behind him. I was from the streets too, the South Bronx, and I wasn't easily intimi-dated. I was perfectly comfortable adding a little bass and swagger since I was surrounded by fourteen para-military type security guards armed to the hilt. Not to mention Missy Elliot's two mammoth-sized bodyguards who were keeping an eye on the situation. The chief of police asked me if he needed to step in, I told him I was good but we all watched as C-Murder and his ragtag

I ENVISIONED MYSELF SITTING IN BOB JOHNSON'S (CEO & FOUNDER OF BET) SEAT ONE DAY.

crew left the VIP entrance area. You can never use too much force with wannabe rappers. Violence can break out at a moment's notice. Years later, I learned that C-Murder was actually wanted for murder.

During the few years I spent overseeing Spring Bling, I became good friends with Ray J, a rising rapper, singer, and actor whose famous sister, Brandy, was killing the R&B charts. Ray J was one of our featured hosts for the event and he was doing a bang up job keeping the audience engaged and the show on schedule. Thanks to my new buddy, the show was an overwhelming success and earned a nice little mint for BET. A few months after the show aired, I was taken aback when Ray J reached out to me and invited my wife and me as VIP guests for a surprise birthday party he was throwing for his sister, Brandy. My wife was shocked that a limo picked us up and was more surprised when I was invited to dance with the birthday girl, Brandy. Years later, I was surprised to hear about the sex tape scandal with Ray J and Kim Kardashian, which propelled the Kardashian family into the celebrity spotlight overnight.

As BET's Assistant Deputy General Counsel, my duties included managing insurance, compliance, trademarks, *BET news, HITS from the Street, Teen Summit,* and general litigation. My immediate supervisor in the legal department was a Navy Seal Captain, who could probably annihilate someone with his pinkie finger. A phenomenal boss, he embodied autonomy and creativity. I knew if I played my cards right, I'd be able to quickly rise to the top. I envisioned myself sitting in Bob Johnson's (CEO & Founder of BET) seat one day. While channel surfing in my office one morning, I was captivated by a beautiful black reporter named Jacque Reid. I said any person who was exciting enough to get me to watch the news might be a great fit for BET News. Coming off the negative press after the firing of popular host Tavis Smiley, BET needed a breath of fresh air, and from what I had seen, Jacque appeared to be just what the doctor ordered.

I immediately called Michael Fountain, head of BET News, and asked him to turn on CNN. He agreed that she would be a real asset to BET's News program. I took the initiative and called CNN and asked for Jacque and was told she was still on the air. I agreed to hold for her until she was available. Our initial conversation went a little like this: *"Ms. Reid, this is Thomas Felder, I am an attorney for BET and our network is considering bringing you on as our primary correspondent. If we can work out a mutually agreeable deal, would you be interested in joining us in Washington D.C.?"* She sounded very interested and gave me a quick, *"Yes."* After making Jacque an offer she couldn't refuse, she joined BET forty-five days later. Thanks to my eye for talent BET News enjoyed its highest rating. Jacque quickly became a household name. I had hoped I'd be rewarded by a quick ascension up the executive ladder.

In addition to my suit and tie gig at BET, I was responsible for babysitting one of our hottest celebrities in Hip Hop; a very talented comedian named, Hits. Hits had a show called, *"Hits from the Street."* Hits would play practical jokes on unsuspecting victims in public. The show had incredible ratings, but the company was always moments away from a major lawsuit every time Hits stepped out of the building. He was often called a menace for the practical jokes he pulled on ordinary Joes and celebrities he came in contact with. While I thoroughly enjoyed my time with Hits, he was somewhat troubling for the network. My newfound friend and I had a blast traveling and touring the country. Every time he got himself into trouble, I was there to bail him out. Some of the most memorable moments I shared with Hits include hanging out backstage at a Prince concert and meeting the Tennessee Lady Volunteers as they prepared to defend their NCAA Division I Basketball title. Other great memories include hanging out with Lil Wayne, Lil John, Snoop Dogg, and many more. With our camera crew in tow, we crashed video sets and parties from coast to coast.

Without a doubt, one of the wildest assignments Hits and I had was our trip to Chicago to film) The Players Ball. The Players Ball was an awards show similar to the Oscars. The only difference between the Oscars and The Players Ball was that the invitees and guest of honor for the Players Ball were actually the most successful pimps in America. The show for pimps gave recognition to the pimps who had the best hair, best cars, most women, etc.

Watching the arrival of the pimps reminded me of the worst portions of two movies, "I'm Gonna Git You Sucka", and "Pootie Tang." Most of the pimps arrived with large entourages wearing bright pink, green, and canary yellow suits, along with their customary matching feather hats. For the life of me, I can't figure out why anyone would make, sell or wear such horrible outfits. For me the icing on the event was watching each player drive up in either a red, green or hot orange colored Rolls Royce. At the end of the day, MTV loved the content of *Hits from The Street*, and came out with a copycat version of the show called, *"Jackass."*

During my [nearly] 3-year tenure at BET, I met some of the most noteworthy black celebrities there are—from Stevie Wonder to Magic Johnson and everyone in between. BET started an AIDS awareness campaign and I was invited to a marketing department meeting where we selected a name for it. The campaign was called, "RAP-IT-UP." I drew up the paperwork and created the largest AIDS awareness campaign in the African American community. We later teamed up with Magic Johnson's foundation to throw a joint fundraiser. During the fundraiser, every black celebrity in the country showed up. Richard Roundtree (commonly known as "Shaft") was there, Mariah Carey, Mary J. Blige, and so many more. All of my colleagues from BET were trying to get close to Magic Johnson to catch a picture with him. It was impossible; only the 'A' celebrities were able to get close. I bet one of my fellow attorneys $1 that I could make Magic Johnson to come across the room and greet us in the next five minutes.

They all laughed and watched as I yelled out, *"Buckey!!!"* three times at the top of my lungs over the loud music being played by Kid Capri. Magic heard me, stopped taking pictures with the 'A' types and made a bee line straight to me. Magic came over, gave me a hug and high five, took pictures with us and hung around for thirty minutes before going back over to the A-listers. Everyone wanted to know my secret. Did I know Magic? I never told them my secret. The fact was I read in Magic's autobiography, which had been released just before the party, that all of his good friends called him *"Buckey"*. I decided to try it out and it worked. My love of reading paid off again.

I was working at BET on the morning of the 911 terrorist attacks. The entire office had televisions and we huddled around frozen in fear that we were under siege by an enemy force. The situation became even more real when one of our staff attorneys called in to say she was stuck on the highway and just watched a plane fly into the Pentagon. She wasn't sure what was going on at the time but said she wanted to head home instead of coming to work today. We didn't know we were in the middle of a crisis that would change the fabric of American Freedom, and thus change the face of America forever. It took a few months before life on the fifth floor was back to normal.

I had the privilege of meeting Stevie Wonder and Luther Vandross when they were honored at BET's lifetime achievement awards show. I was pleased to meet each of them while I held the security and risk management detail. One of the singers slated to perform was Faith Evans, the widow of the late rapper, Biggie Smalls. Faith was up next but she was a bit frantic because her mother and family members had not arrived for the function as expected. As it turned out her mother had arrived in an older model Nissan Altima filled with passengers. No one knew to expect her and she was not listed on any of the VIP lists I was given. Just as an argument was cooling down between the gate security guard and the Nissan passengers, I arrived on the scene and was brought up to speed on what was going on. I couldn't reach Faith directly because she was getting ready for her performance, so I made a judgment call and admitted her mother and the other passengers. I gave them VIP passes, and then proceeded to walk her mother backstage. Faith was ecstatic and gave me a big thank you from the stage after the event. I was grateful to be in a position to help.

BET allowed me to become both a local and national mover and shaker by connecting me with numerous politicians, bankers, and power brokers across the country. Many of the power brokers requested my assistance in raising money for one candidate or another. I went from doing fundraisers for local politicians to doing one for the biggest politician of all. My good friend, Orlan, said we should put together a fundraiser for a black guy running for president. My wife thought it would be a waste of time and reminded me of the Jesse Jackson and Al Sharpton runs. Once she heard that the guy had an African name, she said, *"America is not ready for this yet."* My friend, Orlan, assured me that it was a long shot but it would not be a waste of time. Orlan said, *"I saw this guy work the room as good as Bill Clinton, he is a rock star just wait until America gets to know him."*

PRINCIPLE # 17
EVERY LITTLE BIT COUNTS

In order to build a brick house, you must lay the bricks one at a time. No matter how small your striving may seem at the time or how long it may take to see results it all affects and benefits the change you're seeking and will show results in the end. Stay the course!

Orlan put together a series of fundraisers for this unknown dark-horse candidate. We rented the Columbus Club in Washington D.C.'s Union Station and held a who's who fundraiser that brought in close to $300,000 for Senator Barack Obama. At our first meeting, there were no secret service agents because at least ten candidates were running for President. Over the next three months, I had the opportunity to meet with Senator Obama on five different occasions. I was happy to be of service as he climbed the political ladder. He later thanked me for my fundraising efforts when I met him at a California fundraiser hosted at Oprah Winfrey's home. In attendance with us on the lawn at Oprah's house, was Denzel Washington, Shamar Moore, Whitney Houston, Lou Gossett,

Jr. and every celebrity and sports figure on my *"I must meet before I die* list." My wife now sports her picture with President Obama in her office as a reminder to everyone that she knew him before he was famous. I'm happy to say that I was glad to play a small role in helping him raise money for his campaign and go on to a second term.

After my first year at BET, I was tasked with working secretly with one other attorney on the sale and merger of BET to Viacom. Viacom is one of the largest television programming conglomerates in the world. They own CBS, MTV, Nickelodeon, CMT, and ten other networks each being multi-billion dollar enterprises. I was assigned by BET to negotiate every detail of the merger along with an army of lawyers in New York and Washington D.C. For sixteen months, I worked seventeen hours a day determining what was going to be sold, what was going to be spun off, who would stay, who would be fired, what facilities would be shut down, and so on and so on. I knew who was getting what severance package, and knew that it was just a matter of months before hundreds of people I knew and liked would be unemployed. I knew... but they didn't. I wasn't allowed to tell them because the deal wasn't final. As a result of the deal, Bob Johnson became the second black billionaire in America. Mr. Johnson won in the deal, but the employees lost.

The firing and layoffs began as soon as the last document was notarized. Each employee held the belief that they were too valuable to be fired. Everyone appeared unaffected because they thought they were protected by their unique job description or tenure. They didn't understand that Viacom had hundreds of people who could and would gladly do their irreplaceable tasks. After the merger was completed, I resumed a more reasonable 13-hour work day. I was so wrapped up in lead-

> **I WAS IN TOTAL SHOCK AFTER LEARNING VIACOM HAD 400 IN-HOUSE ATTORNEYS AND MY SERVICES WERE NO LONGER REQUIRED.**

ing BET transition efforts that I was caught completely off guard when I discovered that I, too, would be a casualty of this merger. I was in total shock after learning Viacom had 400 in-house attorneys and my services were no longer required.

PRINCIPLE # 18
ANYONE CAN BE REPLACED

Unless you are working for yourself, never feel that you are irreplaceable. Anyone can be replaced, unless you write your own paycheck.

One week prior to receiving my pink slip, I was celebrated for doing such a great job on the merger. I was a victim of my own success. The BET camp was in shambles; each day there were fifty security guards everywhere packing up offices and escorting people off the company premises. The employees knew what was coming but they had no place to go and no back-up plan. So, as time progressed, they went into a state of depression. They'd watch TV in their offices and wait for their termination walk. They went from six-figure salaries to a six-week severance package overnight.

Most people thought they were indispensable because of their title or position within the organization. It was a cruel awakening for many who'd been there since the founding of Black Entertainment Television. While many of the employees were panicking, I kicked into survival mode as I'd always done. The entrepreneur inside was sleeping but not dead. I took my severance package and started my own law firm for the second time. This time I also started a title company, restaurant, and got a realtor's license. I didn't know what the future would hold but I hated feeling financially vulnerable. I could have looked for another top tier corporate opportunity, but I am not a big fan of putting my financial life in some-one else's hands. No one has a more vested interest in my wife, household and children than I do. I figured if the boss was willing to pay me six-figures then what must I really be worth?

PRINCIPLE # 19
FREEDOM OF THE MIND

Not everyone is built to be an entrepreneur, but you should at least value your worth. So many people find contentment with their salary, but never ask what they're making the company or their boss. Asking these questions is the start to freeing your mind and exploring the idea of entrepreneurship.

I vowed from that day forward to never give up my free-dom card again. If I was ever going to live the American Dream, it was up to me no matter how tempting the offer might be or how cushy the job was. J.O.B. to me, means Just Over Broke! You work in an environment where you do just enough not to get fired and your boss pays you just enough for you not to quit. I was born for a life worth more than just enough. I am an eagle born to soar and dominate my borders. An eagle mindset is necessary if you want to leave the turkey-coop mentality of having to take anything that comes your way.

CHAPTER 7

"THE NEW DEAL"

The fools in life want things fast and easy — money, success, attention. Boredom and fear are their biggest enemies. Whatever they manage to get slips through their hands as fast as it comes in. You, on the other hand, want to outlast your rivals. You are building the foundation for something that can continue to expand. To make this happen, you will have to serve an apprenticeship. You must learn early on to endure the hours of practice and drudgery, knowing that in the end all of that time will result in greater satisfaction. Your goal is to master your craft and reach the ultimate skill level where you will have an intuitive feel for what must come next.
MASTERY - Robert Greene

Daughter: *"Daddy, please come to my basketball game it's at 5 p.m."*

Me: *Okay, I'll be there.*

Daughter: *Really, daddy? You always say you're going to make it but you never do… something always comes up.*

The season was ending and my daughter was in the finals and I finally decided to surprise her and make it

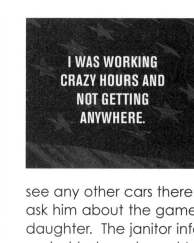

I WAS WORKING CRAZY HOURS AND NOT GETTING ANYWHERE.

to her game. I missed three prior games I had promised to attend. I felt awful about that and was determined to make it to this one. So, there I was; I was even early. The game was due to start at 5:00 p.m. and it was only 4:30 p.m. Strangely, I didn't see any other cars there. It was just me and the janitor. I ask him about the game schedule and if he'd seen my daughter. The janitor informed me that the season had ended last week, and I missed my daughter make the game winning shot.

It hit me like a ton of bricks. I let my little angel down. Enough was enough. I was working crazy hours and not getting anywhere. My cases were burying me, I was gaining weight, going bald and my stress meter was officially off the Richter scale. I thought I would take a minute and try to connect with my kids especially my daughter during her basketball tournament, but my schedule was so erratic I could barely keep up with myself. I am so thankful that my office was on the second floor and not the fifth, because that's probably the only thing that kept me from jumping.

I had employees but I sure didn't feel like the boss. I was left to juggle the bills, taxes, unemployment, lease payments and don't mention health care benefits. Vacations were out of the question. When I did go on vacation, I was afraid to get in the water because I couldn't bear to be separated from my cell phone and miss that all-important client. A few of my employees would regularly miss work—depending on the weather. If the weatherman said there was a 50% chance of rain, there was a 50% chance that LaKisha was going to miss work.

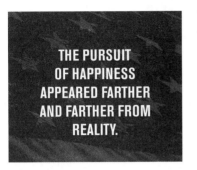

THE PURSUIT OF HAPPINESS APPEARED FARTHER AND FARTHER FROM REALITY.

This hellish work schedule was putting a strain on my marriage. Did I even still have a marriage? Whenever I had a minute to be with my wife, I was completely exhausted. Forget romance, couldn't fit it into the schedule. I went to read my kids a bedtime story and fell asleep on page one. I considered bankruptcy but I was making too much to file or should I say I was too prideful to file because I filed over a thousand cases for my clients and knew the judges personally. I was boxed in on every side.

If I was feeling that kind of pressure with a decent six-figure income, what was the average American going through? What kind of hell were they catching? I felt trapped in some vicious cycle where I Work to GET PAID just to PAY BILLS then back to WORK to GET PAID just to PAY BILLS then back to WORK. It was a never-ending cycle; like going around on a hamster wheel with no end in sight. There had to be a better way, a different paradigm. This madness was not the American Dream. This was not why millions of people risked life and limb to come to this amazing country. Sometime in the last 200 years, the American Dream started slipping away, along with school, multiple degrees, two-income households, voting rights, benefits and 401k's. Nothing was in place to restore the dream. The politicians have lied to us and we've bought it hook, line and sinker. The pursuit of happiness appeared farther and farther from reality.

For the average American, an office or cubicle has become a prison cell where we will likely serve a 40-year sentence. We're allowed to visit our families in the evening only to return in the morning. We know our bosses and co-workers better than we know our children and spouses. There is no expectation of early parole. In fact, the parole date based on the depleted social security accounts have been pushed back another ten years or so; meaning, we have to survive until age seventy or eighty to see the light at the end of the tunnel.

Once our bosses have taken the best years of our lives and energy, then we can vacation and see the world with a walker or cane. We can bond with our spouse, that is, if our marriage survived or if our spouse is still with us. And of course it's too late to mentor our children, but at least we can spend our waning years with our grand-children. This wouldn't be half bad except that most re-tirees at seventy or eighty are taking on second jobs and new careers because they can't live on 40% of what they were making before they retired, and they prefer to pass on eating dog food.

On November 13, 2011, a good friend of mine, named Jay, invited me to try out a credit card swipe machine that he insisted would save me $.09 per transaction. I told him I was too busy to consider his product and blew him off. Jay was a former running back for the New Jer-sey Generals, one of the leading USFL teams from back in the 1980's. Jay played the same position as Herschel Walker, one of the greatest football players ever. Playing backup to Herschel was like being the backup shoot-ing guard to Michael Jordan. In addition to his strong athletic presence, Jay was a Princeton graduate who became a trading manager for Merrill Lynch. Jay was a former client who became a friend. He owned all types of businesses, from hotels to restaurants to nightclubs. He was also a developer for million dollar real estate proj-ects. Jay started his own energy company to supply corn ethanol E-85 fuel across the country. He had the Midas touch and I was grateful to have him as a mentor for any business venture. He always knew how to find the best deals and moved on them quickly while most people were still trying to get a grasp of the deal or the numbers. Jay was a rare mix of human calculator and pit bull. He knew how to make sense of a deal and close it.

Never one to quit, Jay stopped by the office the next day. It was freezing cold, dark, and raining, yet, he insisted I go with him to meet a barber who used to be one of the country's best and brightest boxing promoters. Jay told me Don King mentored the barber personally and the barber formerly represented Mike Tyson and Laila Ali. Additionally, the barber's wife was a beautiful but lethal 5-time world champion boxer herself.

After years of being Jay's friend and attorney, I surmised Jay was about to drop something big on me. I could feel it. I was glad that I would have the opportunity to partner with him on one of his ventures. Jay picked me up in his Hummer just before 7:00 p.m. We quickly rushed out of my office with excitement and urgency, jumped in his Hummer and proceeded to meet the barber. I thought Jay was going to enter the fight game and bring a big name fighter to the Maryland Casinos. I was expecting to be his lawyer, business advisor, and maybe even a partner in the deal.

About ten minutes later, we arrived at a plush, gated community where we had to be buzzed-in to enter the development. In a community of lavish million dollar homes, this house stood head and shoulders above the others. The lawn was manicured, not mowed. As we drove through the roundabout, Jay hopped out of the car and rang the doorbell. I was mesmerized as I looked at the string of BMW's that lined the driveway.

I stepped into the house and into a 20-foot foyer. I smelled expensive perfume. I smelled flowers. I smelled spices and herbs like a meal was being served. I saw original artwork and statues beneath the chandeliers. The barber's wife, who could have been a James Bond vixen, beautiful and deadly, greeted Jay and me. We were escorted to the lower level of the house. There were about fifty people in the room, maybe they too were investors in this dream deal. The meeting was already in progress. I was not sure what I missed and supposed the presenter was going over the finer points of the deal. I put on my legal cap so I could focus and evaluate the terms being offered; I would give Jay my best advice.

I pulled out my legal pad and slipped into a seat at the back next to Jay. Once I was seated and focused on the presenter, I immediately noticed the room was full of prospects. There was a pretty lady in the front of the room selling something, but I couldn't figure out what it was exactly. She was giving the breakdown of the company history, leadership, and benefits. I still didn't know what the product was and I was getting annoyed. I didn't know if the product was water, vitamins, Tupperware, lotions, potions, pills or girdles. I wanted her to stop dragging it out and get to the point. Whatever it was, I wanted to get it over with and go home. For the last fifteen years, I'd been working 15-hour days—winter, spring, summer, fall, so I didn't have any time to waste or mess around. Despite my initial instinct to bolt out of that place, I tried to pay attention. Jay was sitting in rapt attention like we were in a church pew, so I tried to be patient. Jay wasn't one to waste time either and since he was listening attentively, I thought I should at least sit still for another thirty minutes before I insisted on leaving.

It was already after 7:30 p.m., it was late. I was hungry, tired, and grumpy. I'm not usually grumpy but I'd had a long day in court. I was the trial lawyer on a case that had gone on for days and millions were at stake. The parties were in a heated battle and my reputation was on the line. Just before Jay picked me up, I was rushing to get home to attend to my daddy duties.

By 8:00 p.m., I was still waiting for the lady to conclude her presentation. I crossed my legs in the power-leg-cross position and my arms were crossed too. With each minute ticking on the clock, I was becoming angrier and more uptight. What was the point of this foolishness? What started out smelling like roses was starting to smell more and more like a rat! What did I get myself into? I'm sure I crossed my eyes and definitely shut my mind. Nothing happening there that night was going to change my disposition. I just wanted to get out of there ASAP.

Just as I was about to storm out, Mr. Dapper Dan himself, the barber decided to grace us with his presence. The pretty lady who had been talking for the last forty minutes was the pre-act, the opener to the real presentation. The barber was slick and set us up for the big act in true promoter type fashion. With flair and vigor, the barber took charge of the room. He spoke with passion and conviction, and the tone of the room went from a business meeting to a revival as the barber laid it down like Reverend Jimmy Swaggart. The barber spoke with all the passion of Thomas Jefferson speaking of independence, Lincoln speaking about the Emancipation Proclamation, and King giving his, "I Have a Dream" speech. This guy was no joke. He was smart, energetic, and fervent about this presentation. The barber was the real deal, this wasn't an act.

PRINCIPLE # 20 - KEEP AN OPEN MIND

Some opportunities take a little longer to manifest. It's important to keep an open mind to new ways to advance your life.

I had a change of heart and listened earnestly as he broke down the business model. He spoke candidly about the pain of losing a bundle in real estate and other ventures. After Mike Tyson got knocked out and Laila became pregnant, he was experiencing a severe cash crunch. He explained how the company he worked with afforded him more comforts than the fluctuating income from promoting Iron Mike. The barber explained to me that in just three years of working in the network marketing industry he was exceeding my attorney income monthly. To add insult to injury, he told me that he worked from the comfort of his own home for about two hours every day. Prior to this night, I had never really known anyone who was successful at network marketing with the exception of my childhood friend, Roger, who never taught me the secret of his success. The barber captured my attention and imagination. Here I sat with more degrees than a thermometer and I'd never been taught the power of residual income and its ability to create wealth exponentially. The barber had swag, spoke with confidence, and in one instant I began to dream again. He told me that he got up when he was finished sleeping and his children didn't have to go outside their front door for a role model. He had the ability and luxury of staying home all day and was the only dad in his children's school that could attend every school field trip.

This guy told me how he set records in this business and I believed him. So once again, just like when I mirrored

> **I SAW AN OPPORTUNITY AND WENT DOWN TO THE FRONT OF THE ROOM LIKE A CONVERT AT A REVIVAL.**

Lynnette's success, I would model my efforts after him in the same way that I trained for the Marine Corp marathon with the goal of beating Oprah's time. If he could do it, then I could do it. I started my mantra again; anything he could do I could do better, anything you can do, I can do too. The song that I loved so much as a child started to play involuntarily in my head. As calculated as the closing argument of Johnny Cochran to the jury for O.J., the barber turned to us and asked did anyone see an opportunity for themselves, and if so come down. I saw an opportunity and went down to the front of the room like a convert at a revival. I was sold. I filled out the application and I was going to find out if the preacher and this business was real or just smoke, mirrors, and promoter hype.

I headed home with notes on my legal pad about the business, unlimited earning potential and breaking the barber's record. The next day, I started carrying around a 4-foot white board to track my progress. By writing down my goals, I harnessed a subconscious power that allowed me to focus and draw on my reserved willpower every waking moment. Daily I reviewed and updated my goals to stay on task. I was like a runner who knew the 4-minute mile could be accomplished because Roger Banister broke the 4-minute mile barrier. Before Roger, the 4-minute barrier had stood for a thousand years for Olympian caliber athletes. However, once the barrier was broken, the impossible became possible and the possible became probable and the probable became likely, and the likely became inevitable. I wanted the barber's lifestyle and I was willing to walk on water or run through fire if this business was legal and ethical.

I WAS EITHER GOING TO BE THE BIGGEST SUCCESS OR THE BIGGEST FAILURE IN THE COMPANY'S HISTORY.

There's a saying that, *"Once your mind expands, it can never go back to its original position."* I don't know who said it, but it's true. My mind was racing a million miles a minute. I didn't know whether I should step out into the business that quickly. But I was going from being skeptical to the max to being "all-in" in a matter of minutes. Before the barber finished presenting, I decided I was all in; it was my chance to regain my sanity. The legal profession was burning me on both ends and in the middle. Some of my clients were ingrates; others were almost vampires sucking my blood. My profession, which used to be a source of joy, became a labyrinth of deadlines, filings, long nights, bad diets, tension, and mental, physical, and spiritual exhaustion.

If life was my Titanic, this business was my life vest. I was making good money but I was overwhelmed by debts created from the down economy and toppled real estate market in which I was highly vested. I had mortgages that were due, tenants who believed they were entitled not to pay their rent, and a long list of legal clients who were dodging my invoices like the plague. Everywhere I turned, I felt trapped. I was drowning.

In the back of my mind, I heard the Lord whisper in my ear, I sent you to look at this business to rescue you. So I decided to jump in 10,000%, I was either going to be the biggest success or the biggest failure in the company's history. Either this business was going to work or it wasn't. I was comforted in knowing that Robert Kiyosaki wholeheartedly endorsed network marketing and stated that it was one of the best means of obtaining substantial wealth. I didn't need a six-figure income to address my seven-figure debt, I needed a miracle and I needed it yesterday.

It is the moments when we become comfortable that we are the most vulnerable. Being content with your current position is dangerous because the cycle of life and of business is and always will remain in a state of constant change. If you stand still, technology will pass you, life will speed on by, and the fact of the matter is that catching up is exponentially harder than keeping up or even staying ahead. I urge you to stay alert and aware of your surroundings; keep an eye on those who participate in the same rat race you are competing in. Identify the most successful people and businesses in your market, incorporate their positive habits into your daily routine and learn from their mistakes. Most important of all... Remain focused on moving forward instead of reacting to being behind.

By Chris Moore – Social Media Guru

CHAPTER 8

"NEW BEGINNINGS"

I made some immediate decisions that were painful but necessary. I decided to shut down my law office of fifteen years. Many of my friends, family, and new business partners thought I had lost my mind. However, I knew my success in this new venture would take wholehearted commitment; anything less than me giving 10,000% would be a waste of time. I learned early in life that to be successful, *laser focus* is key. I would not get a second chance at this business so I needed to get off on the right foot. Shutting down my office on such short notice was not without many painful consequences, but my new start was a life or death decision for me. My current circumstances were torture and would lead to slow painful death.

PRINCIPLE # 21 - CHOOSE LIFE

When you're living in a situation that can become hazardous or deadly, you've got to choose life. Choosing life can be a painful process but like child birth the pain is only temporary, and the reward is a beautiful new life.

My legal practice was not always so painful, but four things happened in short order, which stole my joy from the profession. First, my sister was attacked, almost fa-

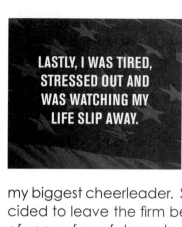

LASTLY, I WAS TIRED, STRESSED OUT AND WAS WATCHING MY LIFE SLIP AWAY.

tally, by her ex-boyfriend. This was bad all by itself but my sister was my right hand at the office. She was my bookkeeper, scheduler, handled my investment properties, and was my business partner. But more than that, she was my friend and my biggest cheerleader. She survived the attack but decided to leave the firm because she needed a change of venue for safety and sanity.

Second, my other office assistant was diagnosed with a serious medical condition and could no longer provide the same level of support. If this was boxing, I was hit with the combo, the old one-two-punch. One to the head followed by one to the gut. Even a great fighter who can normally take a lot of punishment will throw in the towel when he loses the will to fight.

Third, my lease was up on my law office and I didn't want to renew the lease because it was too expensive in the down economy. Who pays $10,000 a month in rent for less than 4,000 square feet of office space in a down economy?

Lastly, I was tired, stressed out and was watching my life slip away. Just yesterday (figuratively), I watched my daughter take her first steps. I blinked and she was twelve years old. I was afraid to blink again for fear she might be all grown up and married. I recalled saying, *"Come here kid"* and she said to me, *"I'm not a kid, kids are baby goats, I am a tween."* I wasn't sure what a tween was but I didn't like the sound of it.

I needed to get my time back right away. I was willing

to climb Mount Everest and back to get it. If you get sick and the Lord heals you, you can be made well. If you lose your money due to the economy or bad decisions, you can eventually get your money back. But, the one asset that is non-redeemable is time.

The pressure and stress I was under was like an elephant sitting on my chest. I couldn't breathe and the weight of the world was on me. I started reading my Bible with renewed vigor and memorized Jeremiah 29:11, which says, *"For I know the thoughts that I think toward you, says the LORD, thoughts of peace and not of evil, to give you a future and a hope."* NKJV.

Reading that Bible verse would give me some comfort that everything would work out somehow. I couldn't hold back my tears; I fell to my knees, huddled up tight and prayed until I fell asleep.

I woke up clutching my chest and thought I was having an asthma attack. It had been years since my asthma bothered me, so it must have been stress induced. I had to get control. I kept thinking about my law office mortgage payment of $10,000 a month, my Amex bill which was nearing $50,000, my car notes of $1,500, my home mortgage and the mortgages on my ten investment properties that I was carrying while my trifling tenants were ducking and dodging service of process on eviction notices. Some tenants bolted and left my houses in squalid states of disrepair. In addition, there were properties where thieves broke in and stole the appliances and pipes. The real estate investing really set me back like many Americans, but I was trying to get my piece of the American Dream and I believed if it had worked out as planned I would have been hailed as a real estate magnate; the next Donald Trump.

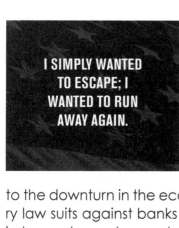

I SIMPLY WANTED TO ESCAPE; I WANTED TO RUN AWAY AGAIN.

To add to this mix, there were open cases and matters with the law office and Title Company and other business dealings where I was being double-crossed by some once loyal business partners. The title company came to a crashing halt due to the downturn in the economy and the rise of predatory law suits against banks to stop foreclosures. I invested in two restaurants so as to not put all my proverbial eggs in one basket.

The mortgage companies would not refinance my properties because they were investment properties and I did not fall under the terms of the sham bank bailout, and I had already renegotiated my office payment twice but it was still too high. When I tracked down a few of my friends who had borrowed large sums of money from me during my heyday, they went into the witness protection program.

I felt trapped again just like I did when I was seven years old. I simply wanted to escape; I wanted to run away again. However, running away was not an option so I dug in and started to grind. So the skeptical lawyer threw caution to the wind and decided to run into unexplored territory like a slave running into Harriet Tubman and discovering the Underground Railroad. *Free at last, free at last, thank God Almighty, I'm free at last.* The skeptical lawyer, who sat in the back, decided to get in the business.

As I started on the new journey I moved with the kind of urgency of a quarterback who was tired of being pounded by a full on blitz. No games... everything was on the line. I had a limited window of time to make this venture work. My reputation, my marriage, and my finances were all on the line. Once I shut down the law practice and my other business ventures, my income stream would dry up in a matter of weeks, not months. When I was jumping into network marketing, I was told that it could take years before I saw a modicum of success close to my attorney income.

Within the first four days of my new business venture with Jay and the barber, I shared the business with over fifty of my closest friends and associates. No one was interested in the business not even remotely. I pitched the idea of working from home to family members. I talked to people who had lots of money and I spoke to people who owed me money and were bound by debt. I was met with *"No"*, *"Nada"*, *"Not interested"*, *"No time"*, *"No money"*. I heard a lot of dial tones and saw a lot of slammed doors. I did my best to mimic and parrot the barber. I tried to imitate his zeal, but still no luck. Maybe I bit the hook too fast. Maybe I was tired and lost my senses when I joined this business. It was obvious that there was no way I could expect to build this business. I thought the barber got in early, was a greater promoter, and had a lot of contacts that he tapped into. Before I threw in the towel, I went to the barber's house to confront him and tell him that this business didn't work and I am no salesman.

Maybe I could get a refund of my $249 investment before it was too late. When I went to the barber's house with the defeated look and told him this business doesn't work, the barber laughed me to scorn, the same way you laugh at a little child. Before I could get my anger and frustration out, he said, *"You didn't do the classes, right?"* I had no idea what he was talking about. Before I could say, *"What classes?"* He said, *"You are frustrat-*

ed and you want to give up already." I felt like he was mocking me. He didn't come out and say it but I could read it in his face, *"You're a chump and you don't know how to tough it out."* No time to get caught up with my feelings. I asked him to explain, "What classes?" I asked. He explained that there is a system to the business and the company has some comprehensive classes that would help me understand.

Classes? How did I miss that critical piece of information? I can handle classes, I am a killer student. I got the details on how to get going with these so called classes and I wanted to know if they would make a difference. I started them immediately; they only took three hours from beginning to end online. After I did them once, I did them again and again. After nine hours of reviewing video tutorials, the business started to make sense to me. I reviewed the information from 4:00 a.m. that morning to past 6:00 p.m. in the evening. I now had the information to go with my motivation. The company I joined was a broker and reseller of gas, electricity, cable, internet, telephone, home security, and mobile phones. The best part of the product line up was that most of the products were brokered for and with the top companies in the U.S. Companies like Verizon, Sprint, T-Mobile, Comcast, and the gas and electric companies across the country. The company also had short term plans of launching out internationally and including a line of coffee plus health and wellness products as there were similar companies having abundant success in those markets already and proved to be profitable.

PRINCIPLE # 22
KNOWLEDGE + PASSION = SUCCESS

Having passion, energy and drive isn't enough to be successful in any business. Knowledge isn't enough. You can have all the knowledge in the world, but if you don't have the passion to share it, the knowledge is worthless. When you combine knowledge & passion, you can't help but be successful!

My original excitement about this business was confirmed by my research. I then stayed up a few more hours researching the landmark case of FTC v. Amway. It was a 1974 case where a network marketing behemoth, called Amway, over the course of a 4-year case defeated the U.S. government. The case held determined that Amway wasn't an illegal pyramid scheme and it laid out the rules stating that a network marketing company must have legitimate products that could be purchased by consumers in the general marketplace, and company representatives' income had to be more derived from the sales of products than from the sales of members into the company. These two points are the core foundation of what you can expect to find in a legitimate network marketing company. I then spent a few hours studying the network marketing industry and learned that there were more than 2,000 network marketing companies in the United States in any given year and only 200 of those companies were members of the Direct Selling Association (DSA).

The DSA, located in Washington, D.C., is a trade association formulated around 1910, but has been in its current form since the 1960's. The DSA is a voluntary association

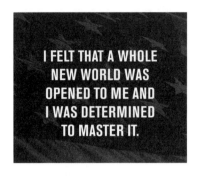

I FELT THAT A WHOLE
NEW WORLD WAS
OPENED TO ME AND
I WAS DETERMINED
TO MASTER IT.

where member companies agree to submit to the highest standards of operation, products, training, and development in their economical and ethical practices in the network marketing industry. I learned that network marketing companies generally fail in the first two to five years. The DSA member companies were not in the trial phase of business and many of them had billion-dollar annual revenues. Not satisfied, I read home business journals, wall street journal articles, and copies of the Inc. Magazine, which praised the network marketing industry and the company I had joined in particular. Hour after hour, I read internet accounts of the top earners in the network marketing industry. I learned of thousands of people becoming millionaires. Many of them from different companies, different products, with high school diplomas, in the U.S. and abroad, some working part time, some working full time.

How could I have missed out on this information for the past thirty years? People have been making six and seven figures a month in this industry. The amount of money they were making was incredible, but what was more incredible was the nominal fees to get started. People could quickly succeed in this industry. Degrees and credit scores were not obstacles. My heart raced and I read book after book about this industry. I felt that a whole new world was opened to me and I was determined to master it as quickly as possible.

With renewed vigor and the music from Rocky's comeback playing in my ears, I called up my sister Denair and told her to get into the business. I told her I can't explain everything right now, I'll email you some videos but we are about to be rich. Believe it or not, my next business partner was easier than my sister. I knew the prospects social security number, where she lived (upstairs), and her application fee was staring me in my face. I took my wife's Amex card and put my wife into the business. She should never have *left home without* it. On my fifth day in the business, I had my first two business partners, my sister and my wife. Neither of them had any idea that they would be at the head of my new empire. I felt like Bill Gates or Steve Jobs putting together my brain trust.

Every day I spent eight or more hours at the barber's house, I was determined to learn this business from the best. The barber mentored me; he was one of the best in the industry. God was looking out for me. If he was going to teach me, I was going to be the grasshopper to the Shaolin Master. I called people all day, I brought over clothes, I worked until I fell asleep and then began again in the middle of the night. I was like the characters in that movie, "Boiler Room". I was grinding in this business as hard as I studied for the Law School Admission Test (LSAT) exam.

It was not unusual that I would push myself to the limit with phone calling, emailing and texting people. If I didn't get 100 *"No's"* by Noon, I wasn't working. This kind of exertion took a heavy emotional toll on me. I would breakdown at least once a week from the pressure. I'd cry, scream, do push-ups, lift weights, watch motivational videos on YouTube, and then I would fall on my knees and pray. I'd ask God for a supernatural intervention. I would get on 5:00 a.m. prayer calls with my mother and family. I learned to pray when I was a kid, it worked then and I would call on God again. I would start doing 6:00 a.m. prayer calls with my newly forming team. Within a few weeks of being in the business, close to 200 peo-

I WAS PLANNING TO, "GET RICH OR DIE TRYING."

ple joined my team and the morning prayer calls were a real source of encouragement for all of us. Preachers and motivational speakers joined us on the call, people like Willie Jolley, Deltorro McNeal, and my friend and publisher, Jeremy Anderson.

Success came to me faster than most because I unconsciously utilized Parkinson's Law as set forth by Cyril Northcote Parkinson in 1955. Parkinson's Law is the adage which states: *Work expands so as to fill the time available for its completion.* In plain language, it means that we can accomplish any task based on the amount of time we allow to complete the task. If you wait until the last minute, it only takes a minute to do. So, with urgency and boldness, I set out on my new path. I didn't care what anyone thought about me, I had made my decision. I was going to push forward with confidence and not turn back no matter what. My decision was swift; it was firm and unwavering. I was planning to, "get rich or die trying" in the words of rapper 50 Cent.

Within a few weeks of being in the business, I hit one of the company's top positions. I was very excited about being promoted, and I immediately looked for Jay to tell him the good news. Upon locating Jay, he informed me that he quit the business. That really threw me off a bit. Quit? What did he mean by quit? Jay is a warrior; a natural born leader, a fighter, football player, and a guy who never gives up. I was really taken aback. I went to see the barber and told him that Jay quit. The barber informed me that his best friend since high school, the guy who hounded him every day for five months to get into the business, quit the business as well.

That's when I came to the realization that people quit on themselves and their dreams way too soon. Immediately after hearing the barber's story, I received a call from one of my new business partners, who was only in the business for five days. He asserted that network marketing didn't work. He agreed that the business was selling products and services that everyone needed, couldn't do without and couldn't payoff even if they were billionaires.   He told me, the business would take too long to build even if it did work. So after only five days of blood, sweat and tears, he was done. After listening to his sob story. I said to him, *"Just Quit!"*

I did not want to convince him to stay in the business, that's not my place. But I asked him how long it had taken him to learn how to ride a bike. He said he didn't know. I said did it take you more than five days? He said, probably so. I said, do you have any children? He said, no. I said it's fair to assume that one day you may have some children right? He said, yes. I said to him how many days are you going to give your kids to learn how to walk? He said, he didn't know. I said do you think you would at least give them five days? He said, yeah. I said what if it takes thirty days? What if it takes two months? How long would you give that kid to learn how to walk? He said until that kid can walk.

So I said to him, you have been in a business that you have the potential of making $20,000 a month working two hours a day. It took you more than five days to learn how to ride a bike and you're quitting on your dreams in five days? But I told him that was quite all right because 99% of all people are Quitters. Yes, they quit! They quit! They quit on everything. They quit on their spouses. They quit on their children. They quit on their jobs, their cars, their pets... they're quitters.

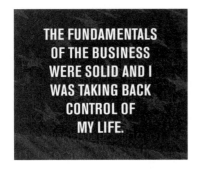

THE FUNDAMENTALS OF THE BUSINESS WERE SOLID AND I WAS TAKING BACK CONTROL OF MY LIFE.

So I told him, 'listen just be like everybody else and just quit!' Then I told him to take his application and put it in a frame and hang it on his wall, and when his children grow up and he's just as broke then as he is now, I told him to point to that frame and say, 'daddy is a quitter.'

If you don't want to do what you need to do to be successful and you are not willing to become uncomfortable, quit! I told that guy if I was a seed or plant in his house he would have thrown me out before I had a chance to grow. I don't have time for quitters because quitters never win, and winners, never quit.

I told my former business partner, that I wasn't just mildly committed, I was fully committed. I told him the fundamentals of the business were solid and I was taking back control of my life. I ended by telling him I felt obligated to bail not only myself out, but share this opportunities with others. After ending my call with the business partner, the barber smiled and shook his head toward me as if to say, you've finally got it kid.

At that time, I didn't know that the time period in which I hit the position was so exceptional. I didn't find out until much later. The barber just kept pushing me intentionally never letting up. He had the competitive spirit of Vince Lombardi, arguably the most revered coach in all professional sports. Mr. Lombardi, often made my accomplishments feel minor so I would stay hungry and on task. When I first joined the business it was in the middle of the Thanksgiving and Christmas holiday season and unbeknownst to me this was supposed to be the worst time to build this type of business. People are not interested in building a business from home when they are shopping, preparing holiday meals, traveling, vacationing and entertaining guests. I put my holiday routine on hold; there was a job to do. My wife wasn't happy and utterly protested. She showed her discontent with my new found profession by bedroom lockouts and threats. No time for that, in my head, I was in Selma, Alabama humming "...*ain't gonna let nobody turn me round, turn me round.*" Bull Connor, fire hoses and German shepherds wouldn't slow me down.

By January of 2012, the company had a major convention in New Orleans, Louisiana where more than 20,000 people were in attendance. I took my last dime and made hotel and airline reservations so I could attend. I invited the leaders of my team because the barber insisted that I be there. I maxed out my credit cards to make it happen. I only had $75 left to my name. Everything else was leverage or held as deposits by the hotel and rental car companies. Talk about putting it all on the line, it was on the line. I was stressed that I mentally went in so hard with no Plan B, but inside I knew that's the only way to win.

The company paid us every Friday and I expected to make a few hundred dollars, which would allow my credit cards to become unfrozen in time to pay for another day at the hotel. I had twelve people staying in my room while I supplemented our diet of hotel lobby apples with pizza pies. At 11:00 a.m. the next morning, it was time to pay for day two at the hotel. The front desk attendant wanted to know if the accommodations were adequate. Next, the manager up the ante and asked whether we needed anything else. With the manager's eyebrow raised, I sensed the only question unasked was, "*Are you ready to pay for tonight's stay or will you be*

WHEN I CHECKED THE ATM SCREEN AGAIN, I FELL TO THE FLOOR AND CRIED OUT LOUD.

checking out?" I knew the credit cards were well beyond the max and in negative territory. I passed my Yankee cap around the lobby, giving my roommates an opportunity to contribute to our stay. I thought I'd allow them to put a little skin in the game. It wasn't looking good; $2, $5, $10 ...uh oh, $0.50. It didn't appear we were going to scrape up enough to stay another day. I was feeling sick and embarrassed. Now what? I was stuck and without options. I refused to ask my wife to bail me out.

With all the confidence of a third-string quarterback, I said a prayer and slipped the credit card to the manager. I was expecting to hear, *"There's a problem"* or *"Your card has been declined."* To my surprise the card went through with no problem. How could that be? I raced over to the ATM, checked the company issued credit card on now my seventh week in the business, and was stunned to learn there had been a $9,000 deposit for the week on my card. This amount was so much more than I expected. I nearly had a heart attack. When I checked the ATM screen again, I fell to the floor and cried out loud. I had never done that before so everyone around me thought I'd just gotten some tragic news, like a death in the family or something. As the tears flowed, all I could think of was the goodness of God. The crowd gathered around to console me. I couldn't find the words to tell them that I didn't have tears of sorrow but tears of joy and validation.

Felder Family Webster Housing Projects In The Bronx

Edward and Mary Felder (Parents) & The Twins (Eddie & Evelyn)

Felder Children and Cousins on Jessup Ave. Denair, Thomas, Lynnette (1st row), Evelyn, Eddie (2nd row), Sonny and Gloria (3rd row)

Felder Children on Jessup Ave. Denair, Eddie, Thomas, Lynnette, Evelyn

Thomas & family Christmas photo. Thomas, Carrington (son), Alexandra (daughter), Adrianna (daughter), Melodie (wife).

Oakwood University Alumni Weekend. Carrington, Alexandra, Melodie, Thomas, Adrianna.

Thomas a Junior at Oakwood University.

Thomas and wife Melodie.

Daughters Alexandra Felder and Adrianna Felder at Disney World.

Alumni Weekend with siblings. Evelyn, Eddie, Lynnette, Denair, Thomas.

Melodie & Thomas at a party.

Thomas & Melodie on a cruise.

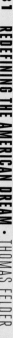

Atlanta. Thomas, Melodie, Denair, Marty Wynn.

Eddie, Carrington, Shon, Thomas.

. Daughters, Adrianna & Alexandra.

Thomas and Melodie,
Bentley Celebration.

Atlanta. Mary (mom), Denair, Thomas.

Bentley celebration with team. Frances, Lajuan, Denair, Melodie, Thomas, Ronda, Owen.

Thomas Felder Anaheim, California.

Thomas 2013 Anaheim, California Promotion Speech.

Thomas & Eddie.

Bentley's & BMW's of top company executives.
Thomas & Melodie far left with Bentley.

CHAPTER 9

"GET IT DONE"

At the New Orleans Super Dome, during the awards ceremony, I was called to the stage nine times during the morning session and people started to ask, *"Who is this phenom? Who is Thomas Felder?"* It was interesting that I spent years behind the scene at BET helping on-stage talent and now in a curious change of circumstances, I had become a mini-celebrity.

By the time the convention was over, I was on a first name basis with every top earner in the company. I was completely stoked about the business. I was determined not to come to the next convention without hitting the next position, which normally took two years to hit. I had less than three months to do it. I went on a furious reading campaign. I read motivational books by Grant Cardone, Zig Ziglar, Jim Rhone, Tim Ferris, and my college classmate from Oakwood, Eric "ET the Hip Hop Preacher" Thomas. I read network marketing books by Eric Worre, Big Al Shreiter, Don Falla, and Richard Brooke. I studied network marketing giants like Dexter Yager, Holton Buggs, Steve Merritt, Brig Hart, Barry Donalson, Steve Carter and so many more. I also studied corporate strategists like Warren Buffet, Robert Kiyosaki, Steve Jobs, and Carl Icahn and others.

PRINCIPLE # 23
KEEP SHIFTING GEARS

Just like driving a stick shift, you can go faster or stronger by shifting into the next gear. If you want to reach higher levels of success, you've got to shift into higher gears. When you think you've exhausted all your gears, you've got to dig deeper, fight harder, sleep less, work later, pray longer, and move faster.

Everything I did initially to build up the business, I quadrupled after my New Orleans success. If before the convention I was making 100 calls a day, I was going to push for 300 a day. If I was sending 1,000 emails a day before, I was now committed to 5,000 a day. If I was texting 200 people a day, I went to 2,000 a day. If I knocked on 20 doors a day, I was now going after 500 doors a day. I was literally on fire; there was no limit to what I would do to get it done. It was time for me to experience success on the next level.

I was more motivated than ever. I was basically living in the barber's sunroom and imposing on his wife and family. Then I tripled my efforts and moved my sister into the barber's house with me. Two weeks later, she relocated her 20-year-old son from Alabama into the barber's house as well. He was a junior in college, working two documented jobs and two undocumented jobs. Just seven days earlier my nephew was thrilled to share that he painted a two story house for just $75. My sister had heard enough, he was definitely looking for an opportunity.

I now had my sister, my nephew, and several of my team members setting up tent city in the barber's house. We

> **IT WAS TIME FOR ME TO EXPERIENCE SUCCESS ON THE NEXT LEVEL.**

were living like vagabonds and doing home meetings almost five or six times a day without stopping. We were presenting in shifts. We did morning presentations for people who worked at night. We did night presentations for people who worked during the day. We had lunch time presentations for anyone who could spare thirty minutes. It was not uncommon for me to be in the same suit for 36-hours straight, napping in between and on the constant presentation grind. We did presentations in the metro, hotel lobbies, Starbucks, at funerals, weddings, graduations, birthday parties, there were no limits. We did it on the internet using Skype, Face time and Google plus.

We drove hours to other states on a moment's notice. We jumped on planes, we got on the Greyhound bus at 1:00 p.m. to go to New York from Maryland to do an evening meeting. We were completely engaged in sharing this wealth-building opportunity.

With the help of the barber's relentless spirit, in just eighty-five days from starting in the business, I was awarded a brand new 5 Series BMW, travel allowances, paid vacations, and 5000 shares of stock in the company. I was shocked when I learned that I had broken a company record in the process. I'd achieved what 300,000 reps in the company failed to do in the company's 12-year history. I picked up the BMW within days of qualifying for it. I liked the smell of it; the leather seats, the sound of the engine. My wife was also coming around, she too was excited. This faith journey was becoming real. I practiced law for more than fifteen years and never owned a BMW. My car prior to hitting this position was a Honda Odyssey minivan. Things were changing. I was starting to see the

I WAS AWARDED A BRAND NEW 5 SERIES BMW, TRAVEL ALLOWANCES, PAID VACATIONS, AND 5000 SHARES OF STOCK IN THE COMPANY.

fruit of my labor. Getting the BMW inspired me to run even harder. It inspired everyone on my team to give more of themselves.

I was excited but I did not stop to celebrate. The journey was just beginning. My sister, Denair, and my nephew Shon, were all the way engaged and we had nightly war-room type meetings. My team and I went from friends to family. I could no longer tell where my family ended and my team began.

I talked to many of my friends and colleagues and one out of every 100 was receptive. With these odds, I was willing to play the numbers. I called people day and night, I emailed, I texted, I handed out fliers and I knocked on doors. I had the urgency of Noah warning the antediluvian world about the upcoming flood. I did not have the luxury of slowing down. In less than three months of running in this business I had made close to six figures and couldn't believe it. I was pressing hard but still had more to give. Once I found out about residual income, I resigned myself to be its champion and ambassador. So many of my friends and family were in dead-end jobs and I knew if they gave my business the kind of urgency and all out effort they were giving to the jobs they would have options and multiple streams of income.

As the strain of building this business mounted, my religious life grew. I named my team, "Team TNT", which represented our strong belief that faith without works is dead. The name was based on a Bible story found in Luke Chapter Eight in the New Testament of the Bible, which tells of a woman with an issue of blood for twelve years. The Bible tells about how this woman risked everything to be rescued. She risked her life and reputation to reach Jesus as he was passing through her town. She could have just prayed and hoped for healing but no not this time. She pushed through the crowd, made her way past Jesus' bodyguards, knelt down and extended herself to reach his garment.

When Jesus realized He was touched, He asked his disciples, *"Who touched me?"* And they seemed puzzled because thousands were pressed all around them. Jesus informed them that the touch He was referring to was not ordinary; it was a touch of faith in action. It was a touch which caused power to be released from Him. The Greek word "dunimos or dynamite" is used in the Bible. The common abbreviation for dynamite is "TNT". The name we chose as a team symbolized our acknowledgment that our success was not solely based on our efforts but our personal activity was necessary to release the "dunimos."

The next few weeks were nothing short of a whirlwind with Team TNT in full force. By May 2012, we blazed a record breaking trail to the next national event in Las Vegas, Nevada. I and many of my team members were acknowledged from the main stage in Las Vegas. We received awards and accolades from the owners of the company and those in attendance. The culmination of the week's events was a speech I gave called "GET IT DONE". The speech was based on a poem by an unknown author. I reworded it to fit the occasion. The crux of the speech came after I was hoisted up on the shoulders of my team members, and elevated ten feet into the air in a metal folding chair. I pretended I was on the royal throne of King Richard the Lionheart.

My, now popular, "Get It Done" speech rang over and

over in my mind as I reminisced about my journey after being introduced to this opportunity just a few short months earlier. Although the multitude of people in the arena sounded like I was dead smack in the middle of a Jets game during the final seconds, I was still able to find a quiet place in my mind that streamed tears of joy at my newfound success and peace of mind.

Introduction by one of the company's Co-Founders:

"We have a gentleman that we are going to introduce that broke the record to Senior Vice President, with no experience. Achieving the position of Senior Vice President in just eighty-five short days, with no experience.

He shut down his law practice of fifteen years before becoming Senior Vice President. His business today has over 6000 customers and over 800 business partners. He credits his success to his wife and his children, who support him in all that he does.

His words of encouragement to you are "Pray like everything depends on God, but work like everything depends on you. Also remember work is hard, this business is easy. " Please help me welcome our newest Senior Vice President out of the state of Maryland...Thomas Wesley Felder.

Followed by rousing cheers, applause and Marvin Sapp's 2008 top gospel hit, *Never Would Have Made It*, echoing throughout the 25,000 plus filled arena in Las Vegas, the already excited crowd grew in enthusiasm as the highly energetic and powerful lyrics of Ty Tibbett rang out with...

"I thought I lost, but actually I won; for by His blood we all have overcome

THAT PLATFORM WOULD FOREVER CHANGE THIS BURNED-OUT ATTORNEY'S LIFE AND EVERYONE I CAME IN CONTACT WITH.

There is no failure, our God can never lose, and that same power, it now belongs to You. Now it's time to celebrate all banners raised, I've got the VICTORY, the VICTORY"

This sent the crowd into a euphoric frenzy because they also wanted victory in achieving the American Dream. I strongly believe that God allowed me to obtain this position to lighten the path to freedom for so many others. As I glided up the eight stairs to be greeted by the co-founders with politically correct handshakes, I really wanted to hug all of them at the same time with my extended (stretch Armstrong) arms of gratitude.

I remained composed and reached out for my wife to join me on the stage that resembled a night at the Grammy's with strobe lights roaming, cameras anchored, and photographers capturing me from every angle. That platform would forever change this burned-out attorney's life and everyone I came in contact with.

With my wife by my side, holding an oversized bouquet of long stem roses, waving and smiling as if she were the first lady. A few feet away, stood the dream team; the ones who planted their flags with me from the very beginning starting with my sister, Denair, she was the first, then her best friend Ronda, my sister, Evelyn, my nephew Shon and my brother in law, Darren.

I opened my 4-minutes and 23-seconds speech with...

GET IT DONE

"First and foremost I want to thank God, because without God we cannot get it done. Next, I want to thank the Founders for giving us their vision and making a way for each of us here to get it done. I want to thank all the Platinums and Double Platinums because they have gone before us to show us that it can be done. I want to especially thank Kamila Collier, Marty and Isra Wynn because they are one in a million. I want to thank my beautiful wife because she has stood by my side, she is a wonderful and awesome woman and without her I could not get it done. I'd like to thank my family. I would especially like to thank my team, Team TNT. I would like to thank all of my National Directors, especially the eleven that got it done in under four months. They are awesome and they always Get It Done.

Guys I just want to say to each of you that we are on a road called Financial
Freedom and our destination is a land called, Get It Done.

This road is not straight, it's got a curve called failure, 'cause we've got to
fail our way to the top as we Get It Done.

There are loops called confusion, because you will not understand everything you need to do on day one, but nevertheless Get It Done.

There are speed bumps called friends, and sometimes they are just broke
people keeping broker people even more broke.

And despite your friends you have to do what? Get it done!

Guys there are red lights called enemies, they hate you, they don't want you to get anything done. But despite your enemy you will do what? Get it done!

And guys there are yellow lights called family, and sometimes they are worse than enemies. They won't be your business partner or your customer. But despite your family you will do what? Get It Done!

Guys let me tell you we have jobs, and our jobs are like flats on this road. And jobs if you don't know is, Just Over Broke. You are two minutes from a pink slip, on a job that you hate. So while you are working on your full time job I still want you to do what? Get It Done!

Guys I want to tell you that in the trunk there is a spare, and that spare is called determination, because if your whole team quit like Frank Kimbrough just said you still have to do what? Get It Done!

There is insurance called faith, and a driver named Jesus, and each of us have got to have vision to; Get It Done, Get It Done, Get It Done, Get It Done, Get It Done!

CHAPTER 10

"THE DREAM"

I bounced up and down, and pointed my fingers directly at the 20,000 business partners indicating they had the will and opportunity to get it done as well. With the audience responding to my every question, I suddenly felt what it was like to be a major political candidate delivering the stump speech of his life. The crowd was fired up. I was honored to be able to give a rousing speech that would inspire new and old reps to break their own records and achieve financial freedom. If I could achieve this American Dream so could they. The speech quickly went viral with over 50,000 YouTube views.

Just fourteen months after being awarded a 5 Series I was awarded a 2012 Bentley GT Coupe, along with 5,000 additional shares of company stocks. After being homeless during eight different periods in my life, I was now driving a house on wheels. Sticker price for this four wheel beauty was over $200,000. The picket fence was shattered. If this wasn't the American Dream, what was? I was invited onto the main stage again in November 2012, and shared my success story with tens of thousands of people in attendance.

I told them that for years I was an attorney, and that working fifteen hours a day was not unusual for me. I found myself working on my birthday, Christmas, Thanksgiving, New Year's and I wanted to have more time with

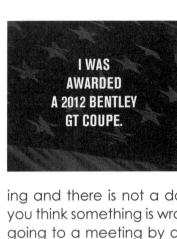

I WAS
AWARDED
A 2012 BENTLEY
GT COUPE.

my family. I realized the one thing that you have that is not redeemable is time; you could never get your time back. My wife had been trained her whole life that you work an hour and you get paid for that hour. So when you talk about working and there is not a dollar for each hour exchanged you think something is wrong. Originally, I was tricked into going to a meeting by a good friend of mine who told me he wanted me to meet someone, and when I got there I saw a room full of people. I was angry and I sat all the way in the back. I was sitting there counting the minutes saying—in thirty minutes, I'm gone. At the last minute I decided I've got nothing to lose and everything to gain.

What I like most is that there is a system that anyone can follow. I don't care if you have a third-grade education, a diploma, or three PhD's from Harvard and Yale, anybody can follow this system. You almost have to make a decision that you want to fail. You've got the chance to do things that doctors and lawyers and people with degrees that have gone to school for years were never able to accomplish. You have time, and you've got money, and you've got them together...what could be better than that?

I always wanted to be a millionaire. Who doesn't want the benefits of financial security? I knew that to be great you must learn to be grateful. This is the only business that I know of where every single person that you run into can be successful. There aren't many of us who are six-feet nine-inches tall. We can't jump over a moving FedEx truck. The older we get the less likely we are to get that

NETWORK MARKETING GIVES ORDINARY PEOPLE A CHANCE TO BE EXTRAORDINARY.

call from the NBA. If you are willing to humble yourself and let your pride go, you can become a millionaire in this business.

Network marketing is a business where I knew that if I gave five to ten years of my life I could not only retire myself, my wife, my mother, but I could retire five generations yet unborn. Most people will never know what it is like to have everything until they are prepared to give everything.

People who want to do something great want to be in a culture of greatness. They want to be led by people who want to win; who are committed to success. If you think about basketball, great players want to play with the Heat, Lakers, Celtics. Those striving for greatness want to play with teams that have a culture of winning even if the team is not having a winning season today.

Network marketing gives ordinary people a chance to be extraordinary. All of us have the chance to be extraordinary. Do you know your life is like a show? You are in a show every single day and I say give your audience something to applaud about. Give them something to celebrate. So often people quit on themselves or refuse to give the necessary effort required to win.

When you work for others, you are at their mercy. They own your work; they own you. Your creative spirit is squashed. What keeps you in such positions is a fear of having to sink or swim on your own. Instead you should have a greater fear of what will happen to you if you remain dependent on others for power. Your goal in every maneuver in life must be ownership, working the corner for yourself. When it is yours, it is yours to lose- you are more motivated, more creative, more alive. The ultimate power in life is to be completely self-reliant, completely yourself.

-By Robert Greene in the 50th Law by 50 Cent and Robert Greene

If you were driving your car and you got a flat, how many of you would get rid of the car? Anybody? That's what it is like when somebody quits on you in network marketing.

If you don't take time to work on your goals and your visions you're gonna spend the rest of your life working on somebody else's. I only have one mantra and it is, "Get It Done." It just means that excuses don't live here. If you are gonna play then play to win. Not everyone that came to the stadium came to win, some of y'all just came to be in the bleachers but if you are reading this book right now...play to win.

The great thing about this business is that it comes with an owner's manual; you're not given the keys to a Lear Jet and told to take off and land the thing on your own. The beautiful thing for me is that it came with detailed flight instructions on how to soar in this industry and be a hero. The company I joined had a presentation which I knew if I learned it well, I could become a millionaire. I knew if people put the same amount of effort and energy into learning the company's training as they would put into an assignment on their job, the amount of effort they put into cleaning their room, the amount of effort you put into a relationship, most people could be financially free.

When I first got into this business I had no success for

> **EVERYTHING I NEEDED TO SUCCEED IN THIS BUSINESS I GOT IT ON DAY ONE.**

the first four days. I thought somehow that I could step into this business and wing it. You cannot wing a multi-million dollar opportunity. On day five in this business I went back to the barber and said *"…this business don't work."* The barber laughed at me and asked, *"Did you do your university training?"* Up until the fourth day in the business, I had not done it, so what I committed to do on the fifth day was to prove the barber wrong. I thought I could outsmart him. So on day five I did my training and my belief system skyrocketed. There was no special intelligence needed. Everything I needed to succeed in this business I got it on day one. There is no room for excuses.

If you manage to wrestle through feeling wildly unqualified to do something awesome, fear will change tactics and hand you a calendar. -Jon Acuff

The barber was a genius he was a great example of what people who are truly committed can accomplish. From the first time I met him, I knew I wanted to share this business like him one day. There were others in the industry that I studied their speeches, their trainings, their work ethic and their integrity.

CHAPTER 11

"THE POWER OF SOCIAL MEDIA"

To consistently build in this business and maintain momentum for years, at times you need to do home meetings. Doing home meetings is your ground game. Any team that is going to become a Super Bowl champion, they need to have a good air game, a good quarterback and they need to have a ground game. A ground game is the running back; they handle the ball. They move the ball forward a little at a time. There are very few teams that can win a championship with just having an air game. The air game if you don't know is the internet and social media.

My greatest breakthrough in network marketing came from a tip from my 11-year-old daughter who recommended that I stop running around like crazy and use Facebook to reach my friends. My daughter said, "Daddy everybody uses Facebook, it's fast, easy, and free." Out of the mouths of babes come the greatest wisdom.

There are more than six billion Facebook users and more than 600 million who check their pages multiple times a day. That very day, I set up a Facebook account and I proceeded to look for and friend every person I ever went to school with. I exhausted my yearbooks from elementary, high school, college, and law school.

Facebook blocked my accounts on several occasions because of the speed I was posting. It's a system to prevent people from spamming. Once I got the hang of social media, I became hungrier and hungrier to reach out to the masses from home. I wish I had utilized social media before now. No matter, after I got the gist of it, I went on a rampage. I set up LinkedIn, Google Plus, Twitter, Instagram, and Pinterest accounts in a matter of days, and reached out to more than 14,000 people about my new business venture.

The internet is the great equalizer. The Fortune 500 companies of the world now have to contend with any Joe Schmo with a laptop and some patience. There are options for people who are stuck in dead-end jobs to thrive in this new economy. All they need is a product to sell and a system to introduce people to that product. The new entrepreneur doesn't even need a unique or original product.

Why Social Media is Important

- Facebook - 701 million. Highest engagement with active users as a percentage of ac count owners at 82%. Domination driven by increased mobile usage and growth by the older demographic.

- Google+ - 359 million. Google+ second largest social network 35% growth in nine months.

- Twitter - 296 million. Charm is being discovered by those in the 55 to 64-age group getting excited about its virtues, fastest growing network with more than a 40% increase in active users over the last nine months.

- LinkedIn is growing at over 30%.

- Pinterest's popularity continues with a 20% increase in active users.

Building my business through social media is very different from a home meeting where you invite friends and family over and talk to them about the business. If you present the business effectively, God-willing, they will join you in your business. When I first got into this business I handed out hundreds of fliers every single day. The fliers simply said, "If you want to learn how to become financially free go to this website and if you like what you see email me back."

I also invited everyone I knew to a home meeting. I started by inviting people I knew and ended up inviting anyone who didn't appear to be an axe-murderer and wanted an opportunity to learn the business. When I first started, everybody I know laughed at me and I was the brunt of many jokes in my community. The jokes ended when network marketing alone allowed me to surpass the incomes of 90% of the nine-to-fivers in America.

My early Facebook Postings:

NOVEMBER 28, 2011 AT 9:53AM

Good morning Facebook family. I hope that all of you had a great Thanksgiving holiday. With the Christmas season fast approaching I would like to offer you the gift of Financial Freedom! Yes, I am now part of one of the fastest growing teams and breaking record numbers. Although I had been introduced to this business over 50 times, I was compelled to join after meeting one of the top earners who asked me to be a part of his team. This electrifying momentum has made a difference in the success of this business.

If you would like to earn enough money to retire from your traditional 9 to 5 please contact me. Feel free to ask me how to become part of this winning team!

This was a Facebook post I did in response to the world allegedly ending on December 21, 2012 based on the end of the Mayan Calendar:

DECEMBER 18, 2012
The world is coming to an end on the 21st (true story):
Are people out there insane? My good friend left a voice-mail that he will get in my business at the end of the year. He wanted to wait to see what was going to happen on the 21st of the month before he got in because he said it's supposed to be the end of the world.

I called him back and asked him if he paid his cell phone and electric bills this month, he said, yes. I told him, great. We have finally found a business where people will pay up even if the world is coming to an end.

He thought that was so funny, he agreed and decided to give me his app tonight. hooray....

OCTOBER 3, 2012 NEAR GREENBELT, MD
LATE NIGHT MONEY TALK - THE DEBATE (Shhhhhh!!!!...in a whisper)...It's past 11:00 p.m. and the 9 to 5-ers should be tucked in about now or still discussing the ins and outs of the debate. I'd hate to wake them from their comfy snooze to tell them it does matter how the debate went if you find yourself laid off tomorrow or fighting foreclosure next week. Both candidates will be gainfully employed despite the election outcome and at least one of them will be in a big white house. It's time for all of us who are still on our grind to debate the real issues like: Can we replace the income from our W-2 employment if the boss pink slips us on a whim? Or can we afford to send our children to college even if they're not on an academic or sports scholarship? Or can we afford to take care of our parents when they have outlived social security or retirement funds? These are the real issues for our COMMANDER IN CHIEF, and until these issues can be

addressed for the masses of the working poor, I suggest that we all get a Plan B. If you don't have a Plan B, take mine. Take a gander at www.tipsbythomas.com

OCTOBER 3, 2012

AND YOU THOUGHT YOU WERE HAVING A BAD DAY.... Last year, my million dollars in property went under, I shut down my law practice, my sister was physically assaulted by an ex-boyfriend, my office assistant was diagnosed with M.S., and I was burned out, exhausted and threw in the towel. I thought no one would ever understand how you could make $30K a month and still be broke. I said God was not fair. Then I bent over to get my shoes so I could rush out of the house feeling defeated and handle my problems on my own. I bumped into my nightstand and my Bible fell on the floor. Somehow the pages flopped open to a verse that said it all. It fell open to Job 1:20-22. King James Version (KJV)

20. Then Job arose, and rent his mantle, and shaved his head, and fell down upon the ground, and worshipped,

21. And said, Naked came I out of my mother's womb, and naked shall I return thither: the LORD gave, and the LORD hath taken away; blessed be the name of the LORD.

22. In all this Job sinned not, nor charged God foolishly. How ironic, God has a sense of humor. Well here I am almost a year later and God is showing off and proving that he can restore the years the locust have stolen, just like he did for Job. Guess what? He can do the same for you. So when you are having the worst day you can imagine, go to Job 1:20-22 and I promise you, you will laugh and say, "It's going to be ok."

Got to go to court today in an hour, already claimed the victory. Claim yours...www.tipsbythomas.com.

CHAPTER 12

"THINK BIG!"

*"If you think the world was surprised when
Nixon resigned,
wait 'til I whip Foreman's behind!"*

*"I've done something new for this fight.
I done wrestled with an alligator,
I done tussled with a whale, handcuffed lightning,
thrown thunder in jail;
only last week, I murdered a rock, injured a stone, hospitalized a brick,
I'm so mean I make medicine sick."*

When it came to catchy rhymes off the cuff, few could rival Muhammad Ali. The 32-year-old Ali was taking on the 24-year-old heavy weight champ, George Foreman, in an October 30, 1974 boxing match dubbed, "The Rumble In The Jungle".

Although he formerly floated like a butterfly and stung like a bee, conventional wisdom held that Ali was going to be beaten to a pulp by Foreman, who had a pretty damaging punch. Long time supporters of Muhammad Ali, including Howard Cosell, feared for his safety. Had Ali finally bitten off more than he could chew? Would the self-proclaimed, "Greatest Of All Time" fail miserably in his quest to regain the heavyweight championship belt that was unjustly stripped from him in 1967, due to his reluctance to fight in the Vietnam War?

By all accounts, it would be a miracle if this Big Mouth, Big Thinker, made it past the second round. Ali's toughest opponents up to that point, Joe Frazier and Ken Norton, had both been knocked out by the massive George Foreman in less than six minutes. After coming out swinging in round one, Muhammad Ali found himself clinging to the ropes; holding on for dear life for the next seven rounds. Although Ali was being pounded relentlessly, he taunted the champ by saying, *"They told me you could punch, George, is that all you got?"* The old guy was simply inviting more punishment! But then, seemingly out of nowhere, Ali delivered a devastating combination... a left, a right, another left followed by an upper cut—in all of eight seconds. Muhammad Ali knocked an exhausted Foreman to the canvas in the eighth round. Against all odds, and amidst pandemonium in the ring, Ali, the Big Thinker regained the title by slaying Goliath.

Ali later revealed he had little to no chance of beating Foreman conventionally. Foreman would simply cut off the ring and overpower him. Instead of battling Foreman toe to toe, Ali allowed the powerful Foreman to mercilessly land hundreds of thunderous blows. Foreman landed so many haymakers that he literally wore himself out hitting Ali.

While Ali was hailed as a tactical genius, the victory of his life was the result of his belief. What separates Champs from Chumps, and lions from lambs is the willingness to Think Big and pay the price for success.

Greatness, for each of us, whether we have the skill of Ali or only high ambition, is based on our belief. I have

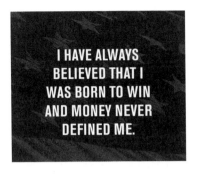

I HAVE ALWAYS BELIEVED THAT I WAS BORN TO WIN AND MONEY NEVER DEFINED ME.

always believed that I was born to win and money never defined me. I have surrounded myself with a Kevlar type faith in the impossible. Most people will never attain even modest amounts of success because they limit what they can do to whether everyone else can do it, and has it been done before. The great ones among us are like eagles that see the world from a different vantage point and are focused on our goals. Those who are afraid to be eagles settle into a comfortable position as clams; forever bottom feeders subject to take whatever life hands them.

For years I thought I was successful; working ridiculously long hours and missing my family who was right down the street from my office. I was like a prisoner serving my 40-year sentence. I knew my staff and clients better than I knew my own family. When I seriously considered that network marketing was an option, I could not rest until I proved that it was a viable business for anyone. If network marketing is not your thing, then utilize the methods and principles in this book to become the master of your universe. Why shouldn't you be a top executive in your firm? How incredible would your life be if you finally completed your degree? How much more would you be able to give to your favorite charity if you were CEO of the next big tech start-up? I know change is not easy, but change is necessary. Embrace the freedom that our wireless and remote society offers us all in the greatest country on the planet. It's time to dream again.

Marianne Williamson said:

"Our deepest fear is not that we are inadequate. Our

deepest fear is that we are powerful beyond measure. It is our light, not our darkness that most frightens us. We ask ourselves, who am I to be brilliant, gorgeous, talented and fabulous? Actually, who are you not to be? You are a child of God. Your playing small does not serve the world. There is nothing enlightened about shrinking so that other people won't feel insecure around you. We are all meant to shine as children do. We were born to make manifest the glory of God that is within us. It's not just in some of us; it's in everyone. And as we let our own light shine, we unconsciously give other people permission to do the same. As we are liberated from our own fear, our presence automatically liberates others."

As a 7-year-old kid in the South Bronx, I was the author of numerous big dreams. I spent hours upon hours in the library reading about people living amazing lives. I told myself, time and time again, I was destined for greatness. At 3:00 a.m. one morning, I threw caution to the wind and took action toward my big dreams and ran away from home risking everything to find something better. For the next thirty-five years I took massive action and refused to settle for crumbs; reaching the top one-percent in elementary school, high school, college, LSAT, Law School, The BAR Exam, and now achieving my dreams in Network Marketing.

As I travel the country sharing my story of success in Network Marketing, I often tell new reps there is nothing special or super human about me. I'm not super-human but I am super-hungry. I tell them there are no short cuts to success, if they want to win big in life and achieve the American Dream they have to be willing to Think Big and Pay The Price. The price for me was rejection from family, friends, and strangers who were ignorant of an industry older than the Internet era. This industry has produced more millionaires than sports, movies, music

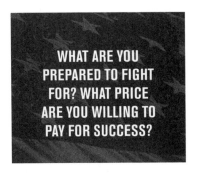

WHAT ARE YOU PREPARED TO FIGHT FOR? WHAT PRICE ARE YOU WILLING TO PAY FOR SUCCESS?

and all of the Fortune 500 companies combined. The pendulum has started to swing and there is a great shift where the nine-to-fivers are looking for the dream. I encourage you to read one of my favorite books, "The 4-hour work week" by Tim Ferriss. The book talks about the shift from working at your office for your boss for pennies to living your life at its fullest and having a full time income on autopilot thanks to the Internet.

While the price for Muhammad Ali's victory was withstanding an onslaught of haymakers from arguably the world's most vicious fighter, the price you pay for success might be as simple as shutting off the television and doing away with Olivia and Scandal. For some it might mean shutting down their Facebook account and setting up an Audible account so you can listen to powerful motivational books on a daily basis. For others it might be getting rid of the clutter in your lives. By clutter, I mean doing away with negative family and friends and replacing them with powerful mentors.

The last time I checked, there were still 24-hours in a day; that is never going to change. The key is to maximize those 24-hours. What are you prepared to fight for? What price are you willing to pay for success?

Think big, take action, and be willing to pay the price. Massive success is an all-inclusive practice. ALL IN! No cutting corners. You'll find that the last pointer is just as important as the first.

PRINCIPLE # 24
VISION! WAKE UP AND DREAM!

We live in the Land of Milk & Honey... America is a modern day promised land. People all over the world risk life and limb to come to our shores. Last time I checked, there wasn't a line of people waiting to go to Mexico, cross the border to Canada or commandeer boats to Cuba. Those who seize the prize focus on what they must do. They don't waste time on things that will not get them to their goals.

To be successful we must focus on the prize not the obstacles. Muhammad Ali said he hated every day of training, but he was willing to do it to be a champion. The media and the 24/7 CNN scare cycle keeps up in fear and doubt of our future. Yes, the world is not perfect, but it is safer and easier now than it has been for the last 6,000 years. The Bible in Proverbs 29:18 says, "where there is no vision the people perish." So I want you to establish a few goals right now. You can write in this book and I recommend that you do. Take ownership of it and your future.

What is the most important thing in your life? Family, job, money, health, etc. What is your "Why"? What gets you up in the morning? To make additional money, have better health, have more time. Having more options improve your ability to focus on your "Why"?

_____

_____

_____

_____

_____

Is your "Why" important enough for you to commit the next two to three years of your life in earnest effort learning and building additional income and opportunities?

_____

_____

_____

_____

_____

You have to face fear like a person fighting for a transplant; no obstacle should stand in your way. Make any and all sacrifices to win. Do the hard stuff. Read the materials. Deal with people who may not be likeable so you can learn what you need to know in order to win. You can no longer walk around with blinders on. Make the world envy; do the bold; walk on water; swim with the sharks. No more could've or should've, it's time to label your list "DONE", "COMPLETED", and "PAID IN FULL" . Today, write one big audacious goal on your mirror (in soap) and commit to give 1000% every day until you achieve it this year. I took on three big goals this year—lose thirty-five pounds, make ten-million this year, and visit three countries with my wife and children in the next 12-months.

_____

_____

_____

_____

_____

What are your big goals? If your goals don't challenge and stretch you to your limit then they are too small.

_____

_____

_____

_____

_____

PRINCIPLE # 25
READ NOT ... WANT NOT!

Reading books is the great equalizer. It allows the common person to reap unlimited wisdom and experience that will accelerate success and learning. In my first 25-months in network marketing, I read more than 100 books written by Network Marketers who were earning over $100,000 per month. I learned from their successes as much as I did from their failures. I did not have to re-invent the wheel. There was already a system in place. Follow it!

According to Jim Rohn, "learning is the beginning of life wealth!" The average CEO reads sixty or more books a year and makes more than 139% of what the average employee earns. Those at the top stay on top because they are the ones with access to the critical information. Read anything and everything about people who are successful in the field you want to dominate. This will motivate, educate, and inspire you to give your all despite any negativity from those who have not tasted success. You can become the Master of your designated universe by reading. If you are not reading, listen to audio books, or free audio downloads from YouTube. In our technological age excuses won't hold up. Buy the books, borrow the books, and get the information to win.

Here are a few books I would recommend to help you along your journey:

- The Bible
- *Think and Grow Rich* by Napoleon Hill
- *How to Win Friends and Influence People* by Dale Carnegie

- *Relentless* by Tim Grover
- *The 4-hour work week* by Timothy Ferriss
- *10 X* by Grant Cardone
- *The 50th Law* by 50 Cent and Robert Greene
- *Secrets to Success* by Eric Thomas
- *The Seasons of Life* by E. James Rohn
- *Mach II* by Richard Brooke
- *Go Pro* by Eric Worre
- *It's Money In The Bank: 7 Insider Tips To Financing Any Small Biz!* By Edward Felder

Franklin D. Roosevelt, the 32nd President of The United States is famously quoted as saying, "Freedom to learn is the first necessity of guaranteeing that man himself shall be self-reliant enough to be free."

PRINCIPLE # 26
UNSUBSCRIBE TO THE LAW OF ONE DAY!

Take action today, not "ONE DAY." There is no such day on the calendar called, ONE DAY. So if you are waiting for "ONE DAY" to be rich, "ONE DAY" to be happy, or "ONE DAY" to be fulfilled "ONE DAY" will never come. Instead of ONE DAY, move with urgency "today", take action right now. Take one step this very moment to move closer to your dreams; make one note, call one person, do one push up. Ideas are worthless until we take action on them. The Bible in James 1:5 says, "faith without works is dead."

Each of us has a window of opportunity ("WOO") in which to succeed. If we don't move when the opportunity presents itself, the opportunity may forever be gone. Many political experts thought Barack Obama should have waited to run for President. He was just a freshman senator and he would be up against the powerful Clinton political machine. He wouldn't have a chance; the United States was not ready for a black president. No waiting for Barack... no "one day". He moved with a sense of urgency to seize his WOO. Today, you and I must seize our WOO. The time is now!!!

PRINCIPLE # 27
CREATE A PLAN & BE WILLING TO PAY THE PRICE

Muhammad Ali in his fight against George Foreman was prepared to sacrifice his body and even his life to be a champion. He was willing to sacrifice his reputation with the chance that Big George was going to knock him out like he knocked out Frazier and Norton. What is your destination and are you willing to pay the price? The price isn't always money, sometimes it's time away from your family. Sometimes it's working harder than everyone around you without any reward or acknowledgment. Paying the price means going forward when those you trust and admire turn back.

Steve Wozniak, one of the founders of Apple, gave a humorous account about when he was in college working for people in exchange for computer parts. Computer parts were more important than money. Steve knew if he could learn to put the pieces together he could make his dreams come true.

When I worked long hours at McDonald's, the Wiz, and even when I wrote books as a kid, I was learning how to put the parts together. As we pay the price by learning from each experience, we can later use those experiences to help us advance when we would otherwise quit. I failed terribly when I took the Law School Admission Test the first time, but I learned how to study the second go around. I knew setbacks would give us the new muscle to press forward as long as we didn't quit.

When you miscalculate the efforts you need to make something happen, you become visibly disappointed and discouraged. This causes you to incorrectly identify the problem and sooner or later assume that the target is unattainable and ultimately throw in the towel...
~ Grant Cardone

PRINCIPLE # 28
ELIMINATE SMALL THINKING

Since you're going to be thinking anyway, you might as well Think Big. We must run toward our goals without limitations. Our limitations are self-imposed. Today refuse to believe you will fail, embrace a vision so big that your heart pounds and you wake up excited every morning.

I dreamed of breaking records and becoming the wealthiest person ever in the history of network marketing. I dreamed of being home with my wife and children, and building our business as a family. I dreamed of seeing the world on my own terms. I dreamed of digging wells so people across the world can have clean water. I dreamed of retiring and being debt free before age forty-five.

To attain my big dreams, I traveled thousands of miles, did thousands of meetings, talked to tens of thousands of people and sent millions of emails and messages, and I would do it all over again. I have been blessed to work with people who share my big thinking. Earl Nightingale said that *"Success is a progressive realization of a worthwhile goal,"* and we should give ourselves time to succeed.

PRINCIPLE # 29
FOLLOW THE LEADER

We can create role models in our mind that can guide us to excellence. As humans we are creatures of imitation, just like ducks. Baby ducklings waddle behind their mothers and imitate every move she makes. We, too, must follow our hero and learn to imitate.

From the time I was a toddler, I was always trying to catch up with the best. I was the youngest of five children and no matter what I did they were bigger, faster, smarter, and all around superior to me in every way. I wanted to be great like my brother and sisters and imitated their every move. I watched my brother play basketball and memorize his moves. I watched my sister Lynnette excel in reading and school work. I would never have attempted to do so well in school without the benefit of her as my role model. I was competing against her but she didn't even know it. The thought that I could catch her pushed me farther and harder than I would have done on my own. Kobe Bryant is in the hunt for his illusive 6th National Basketball Association Championship ring. Kobe's driving force since entering the league as a 17-year-old kid, was Michael Jordon; the guy with six championship rings. Because of Michael's excellence, and his "Just Do It" attitude; there is a Kobe Bryant and a Lebron James in the NBA today. In sports and in business, chasing, mirroring, and imitating the best only makes us better.

When I first jumped into Network Marketing, I was given a 45-minute DVD featuring Steve, one of the top pro-ducing executives in my opportunity Steve was by far and away the best presenter I've ever witnessed. I was spellbound by his eloquence and his presence on stage. Even though I had already joined the company, I was ready to do so again. I watched Steve's video fifty times. I printed Steve's presentation and proceeded to write this entire 45-minute speech by hand twenty-five times. Within fourteen days, I knew every word, smile, hand ges-ture and joke Steve had uttered. He sported light pink ties and handkerchiefs, so I wore pink ties and handker-chiefs. Today, it is a pleasure to join Steve on the com-pany's leader board.

I recommend you find role models in your chosen profes-sion, for your entrepreneurial endeavor, and even in your marriage. Without fail, this simple strategy will lead to you achieving a happier more productive life.

In 2006, although I had never been a long distance run-ner, I decided to run the Marine Corps Marathon in Wash-ington D.C., and I used Oprah Winfrey as my benchmark. Twelve years earlier Oprah had run the Marine Corps Marathon in Washington D.C. When getting up at 3:00 a.m. and 5:00 a.m. in the morning, I used Oprah's 4:29:15 completion time as my yardstick. I was committed to beating the Queen of media. As I iced my sore feet af-ter my daily run, my only thoughts were, I would finally be better than Oprah. I finished the race within minutes of

Oprah's time, despite having three broken toenails and a shoe full of blood, I wouldn't give up. I said, if Oprah can do it, then so can I. I believe if I had targeted actor Edward Norton's marathon time of 3:48, I might have exceeded that as well.

PRINCIPLE # 30
WRITE DOWN YOUR DREAMS AND POST IT

Last year, my wife insisted that the whole family create a vision board. I thought the idea was a ridiculous waste of time. I pushed back really hard, but when it came time to make the vision board I was all in. Seeing my vision in front of me every day gave me the ability to stay focused and on course.

My wife bought picture frames, construction paper, glue, scissors and we allotted ourselves 4-hours to complete the board. I surfed the Internet and pulled out pictures of people exercising and put musclemen on my vision board. I posted a picture of $1,000.000 on my board. I posted pictures of a man and woman vacationing on the beach. I inserted pictures of a brand new Bentley. I put pictures of my daughter playing basketball. While I worked for six hours on my vision board my children and my wife also worked on their vision boards. I am happy to report that vision boards do work. My children and my wife also accomplished each of the goals on their vision board. This year we will create new boards and set even bigger goals. In addition to my vision board, I post signs, pictures and goals on my mirror. It's a long time habit but one that daily reminds me to press forward and never become comfortable.

PRINCIPLE # 31
JOIN MASTER MIND GROUPS

Create a think tank or mastermind group from people who share your hopes and dreams. You can share ideas with people from all walks of life. Most people's income is the average of the five people they spend the most time around.

If the five people you spend the most time with are broke, there is a good chance you are broke too. You can also reap the benefits of surrounding ourselves with experts and skilled people in areas where you are weak. Staying engaged with a mastermind group will keep you engaged on your path. You should have a common goal and regular meetings and activities to keep you on task. With the advent of social media you can reach out to people in other parts of the country or internationally to join you in your quests. I invite you to visit MeetUp. com, establish a LinkedIn Account or join niche groups on Facebook.

PRINCIPLE # 32
FEAR NOT!

True nobility is exempt from fear. ~ Marcus Tullius Cicero

Don't over-think the task ahead, just take one step at a time. When I became overwhelmed with the challenges of a day, my mom would ask me if I could make it one more second. I would say, "Yes." Then she would ask if I could make it one more minute. I would say, "Yes." When I broke the day and challenge down into smaller pieces, I was able to keep moving forward.

We fear things in proportion to our ignorance of them.
~ Christian Nestell Bovee

There are experts who recommend that you tackle the hardest tasks first every day, like in the book, "Eat that Frog" by Brian Tracey. Some experts believe you should take at least one step toward your goal and build on each step. I recommend that you run like a man ablaze with urgency and definiteness of purpose in completing tasks to get the job done. Don't suffer from analysis of paralysis, embrace the journey with positive thinking.

Thomas Edison once said, "Genius is 1% inspiration and 99% perspiration."

PRINCIPLE # 33
MEDIATION AND PRAYER

As I tried to set my mental compass each morning, I had to find true north. I needed to know that there was a higher power guiding my way, and know that I was working in God's will. In Mark 8:36, the Bible says, "What would it profit a man to gain the whole world and lose his soul?" I am a firm believer that people with a center

of faith in a higher power have a deeper well to draw on when there is pressure to quit.

I recommend that you read scriptures daily and engage in at least thirty minutes of quiet introspection. We have to learn to speak to God but also learn to listen. The daily 6:00 a.m. Team TNT prayer call that I host, helps to keep me grounded, humbled, encouraged, and empathetic of others and focused. A daily worship routine will remind you that we are called to do good for others and not just ourselves. We are our brothers' keeper.

I invite you to wake up thirty minutes earlier each morning, and enjoy a quiet walk outside. If it's too cold, I invite you to walk the stairs or hallways of your home. Give yourself permission to Dream and Think Big in this quiet place. This quiet time will provide you with a sense of calm and energize your day.

PRINCIPLE # 34
GO TO SCHOOL

Mark Twain once said, "People who do not read have no advantage over those who cannot read." Invest in your dream by going to worthy conferences and training. Professional development was by far the most critical element in my success.

If you talk to the most successful people, a theme you will consistently hear is that they invest heavily in their success by increasing their knowledge-base. Increasing your knowledge-base is critical to your success. No one will listen to you unless you come across as the expert in your profession or your passion. Ultimately, if you invest in your professional development it will lead to increased confidence in you from others and increased self-esteem.

Today there are hundreds of free webinars, teleseminars, and training all across the Internet. Take advantage of these free resources. Going to school, the investment often outweighs the return. Many times people go to school and take the first job that is offered to them because of the mounting pressure of repaying school loans. There are many non-traditional jobs that have a greater return than the traditional. A college degree offers the person who doesn't have any tangible skills the hope of getting some employment. However, in today's society people are utilizing the internet and social media, learning how to be entrepreneurs and masters of their income. According to the U.S. Census, as of December 31, 2012, the median household income in America is $53,000 and the median individual income is $28,000, which includes a review of more than 114 million households studied.

PRINCIPLE # 35
JOURNAL

Creating a daily To Do List, will help you stay focused and on track. A task list has many benefits. Most importantly, it assists in organizing and documenting tasks that need to be completed daily, weekly or even annually.

Knowing which tasks need to be completed is not enough because to be the most successful, tasks need to be tackled based on their importance. This is accomplished by organizing tasks in the order that they must be completed. If you don't have a task list you will perform tasks without an appreciation for what's most important. Having this kind of system not only prioritizes tasks but the result is increased productivity. Not to mention that it will also help you monitor your success.

PRINCIPLE # 36
AFFIRMATION

Celebrate your success. Acknowledge your good deeds. The way you think about yourself determines what kind of experiences you will have.

Celebrating success is important even before you reach it, because what you think in many situations can determine the outcome of the situation. You have to affirm yourself flooding yourself with positive messages. If something does not go as you planned don't focus on the negative, instead focus on the positive and how you can learn from the experience.

The amount of damage that is done by negative thoughts is immeasurable. Take every opportunity you have to affirm yourself and celebrate what you do right as well as those things that missed the mark!

PRINCIPLE # 37
CREATURES OF HABIT

I can't neglect to mention that if you are trying to develop a new habit, apply the change for 21-days. Research shows that anything you do for 21-days will become a habit. However, habits are only good for as long as you remain consistent, continually applying the new habit.

PRINCIPLE # 38
BE AN EXPERT OF EXECUTION
NOT EXCUSES.

"I complained that I had no shoes until I met a man who had no feet." ~ Persian proverb

If the prize is big enough, there is no obstacle that will stand in your way. Success is mind over matter, if you don't mind then it doesn't matter. For every excuse you can imagine there is someone who overcame the obstacle. Too many are throwing themselves a pity party.

Born with no arms or legs Nick Vujicic doesn't let those details stop him. His courage and tenacity to be all he can be and then some would put most of us to shame. The 30-year-old, whose body make up is primarily centered on his torso, plays football, golf, swims, and surfs.

Although Nick uses a motorized wheel chair, it is not uncommon to see him walking in a waddle like motion balancing himself with his miniature foot on his left hip. And if you think that is amazing, he uses that same one foot to type, write, and pick things up.

Once terrified to live alone, Nick has learned to brush his own teeth with a wall mounted toothbrush. He also washes his hair with a pump action soap dispenser among other daunting tasks we take for granted. When asked how he has the will to survive in a world that is so challenging to him, Nick simply replied,

"I decided to be thankful for what I do have, not get angry about what I don't. I looked at myself in the mirror and said, 'You know what, the world is right that I have no arms or legs, but they'll never take away the beauty of my eyes.' I wanted to concentrate on something good that I had."

With his head held high and a dashing smile on his face, Nick concluded his statement with this: *"I tell people to keep on getting up when they fall and to always love themselves. If I can encourage just one person then my job in this life is done."*

Nick is currently a motivational speaker and has traveled to over twenty-four countries speaking to groups of up to 110,000 people. He has appeared on shows like Oprah, and even has an inspirational DVD titled, *No Arms No Legs No Worries*. Nick is truly the symbol of triumph for people everywhere.

I'm so busy, It won't work, I'm too old, I'm too young, It's raining, It's snowing, It's too hot, It's too cold, I'm too fat, I'm too thin, I'm a single mom, I'm on a fixed income... and drum roll please for my personal all-time favorite

–the dog ate my homework. As ridiculous as some of these excuses sound, millions and millions of Americans use them daily, both consciously and subconsciously, in exchange for not living the incredible lives they once dreamed of. Faulty perception and disparaging myths keep us from believing that we are worthy of the amazing possibilities that lie in wait never to be tapped into.

In my current business opportunity, I had one partner who drove from Maine to Orlando by himself (a 27-hour drive) to attend a national convention. On the flip side, another business partner refused to drive 2-hours to the convention. Who do you think is going to be successful? Who will be the one who makes excuses and never gets it done?

Expect things to go wrong on your journey; it's part of the journey. Murphy's Law is a principle that says unexpected challenges will appear. However, you can overcome Murphy's Law with the law of perseverance, the law of plan ahead, and the law of never give up. Commit to working on your dreams until they are accomplished.

"Luck is the dividend of sweat. The more you sweat, the luckier you get."
~ Ray Kroc

FINAL WORD

"Ideas can be life-changing.
Sometimes all you need to open the door
is just one more good idea".
~Jim Rohn

For as long as I can remember, I've chased the American Dream of prosperity ... "from 9-year-old Brick Layer, to 16-year-old tailor; from Real Estate Investor, to Upscale Restaurateur, I've sought to provide for my family and deliver the "good life." I had dreams of building water wells in Africa and purchasing a home with a white picket fence for my mother. As a result of a chance meeting with a barber with a high school diploma, I am finally on the path to retiring my wife, my children and five generations yet unborn working from the comfort of my living room. That my friend is leveling the playing field ... that is what I call Redefining the American Dream.

W. Clement Stone, who founded a multi-billion-dollar insurance empire with $100, once said, *"If you are really thankful, what do you do? You share!"* I am forever grateful for discovering the keys to unlimited wealth, as such, I am fully committed to sharing this amazing wealth opportunity with all those who dare to dream and think big outside of the box!

If you Think Big, Embrace Social Media, Eliminate Excuses and Fight like hell for two to four years ... I guarantee you'll be able to live life on your own terms. I celebrate you and look forward to meeting you at the beaches of the world.

"You were born to win, but to be a winner, you must plan to win, prepare to win, and expect to win."
~ Zig Ziglar

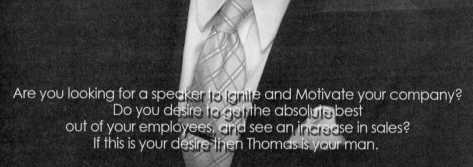

SPIRIT REIGN
PUBLISHING
A Division of Spirit Reign Communications